*e***Shift** challenges us in how to think about and practice ministry in the age of digital networking, social media, multimedia technologies, and mobile devices. No one knows exactly where this techno-cultural epoch is heading, but Posthuma invites us to participate in the conversations that will undoubtedly shape how we respond to emerging opportunities.

—Quentin Schultze
Arthur H. DeKruyter Chair, Calvin College

The church has been choking for decades on the naive assumption that the world hasn't changed. *e***Shift** provides the necessary "Heimlich maneuver" to clear her throat so that the fresh air of life and relevance can return. If you are over forty this writing will be a wake-up call. If you are under twenty-five you will shout "Hallelujah" that someone has finally stated things as they truly are. Either way, *e***Shift** is a gift to the church. Let's hope it's one that is opened and applied, not ignored.

—Dan Webster
Authentic Leadership, Inc., Willow Creek, Crystal Cathedral

eShift

The Decline of "Attractional" Church and the Rise of the
Internet-Influenced Church

David A. Posthuma

CLC PUBLICATIONS
Fort Washington, PA 19034

eShift

Published by CLC Publications

U.S.A.
P.O. Box 1449, Fort Washington, PA 19034

UNITED KINGDOM
CLC International (UK)
51 The Dean. Alresford, Hampshire, SO24 9BJ

Printed in the United States of America
21 20 19 18 17 16 15 14 13 1 2 3 4 5 6

ISBN (Paperback): 978-1-61958-086-2
ISBN (E-book): 978-1-61958-087-9

Contents

Preface

Change never comes easy. Yet change is what *eShift* is all about. As a Reformed Christian, I believe that Christ's church should be in a state of constant reformation. The reformation process is essential to the vitality and relevancy of the church within an ever-transforming culture. Scot McKnight, one of my professors from Trinity Evangelical Divinity School, explains the nature of the transformative impact of the present church movement:

> The emerging movement is consciously and deliberately provocative. Emerging Christians believe the church needs to change, and they are beginning to live as if that change had already occurred.[1]

Indeed, you may find my words "deliberately provocative." I hope, however, that you will filter the words you read through my love and passion for Christ's church. My heart's desire is to support and challenge the church to effectively build Christ's kingdom in this fallen world through proactive disciple making. I believe that our potential for accomplishing our Christ-ordained commission has never been greater.

As you progress through this book and come to distinguish between the established culture and the present emerging culture, you will discover that the differences between these two are profound. Yet I believe that the culture gap can be—must be—bridged, for Christ's mission in this world has not changed nor the power of His Spirit diminished.

Introduction

The Church Confronts Another Epoch

There are certain events that occur so rarely in history that when they do, cultures and generations are transformed for all time. We call these event eras "epochs." An epoch is a cultural advancement that leaves an indelible mark upon the world so that the world is never again the same. An epoch experience is a giant leap in the intellectual and cultural development of humanity. To those of us who have been fortunate to encounter a global epoch and transformed by the experience, we cannot help but view the pre-epoch culture as anything other than mundane and antiquated. This book is about just such an epoch and how that epoch will forever transform the ministry strategies used by Christ's church.

People generally resist change; therefore epochs also are resisted. An epoch is change on steroids, and as such invites resistance from opponents who wish to preserve the previous epoch era. I refer to this principle as epoch resistance. For an example of epoch resistance we need look no further than the invention of the printing press. In general, people within the present era consider the printing press to be an essential mass-communication tool within our culture, even though in many respects the printing press has now morphed into digital print on demand. However, this was not always the case. For example, as one historian tells us,

> Prior to the invention of the printing press, books in Europe were copied mainly in monasteries, or (from the 13th century) in commercial scriptoria, where scribes wrote them out by hand. Accordingly, books were a scarce resource. While it might take someone a year or more to hand copy a Bible, with the Gutenberg press it was possible to create several hundred copies a year. The rise of printed works was not immediately popular, however. Not only did the papal court contemplate making printing presses an industry requiring a license from the Catholic Church (an idea rejected in the end), but as early as the 15th century, some nobles refused to have printed books in their libraries, thinking that to do so would sully their valuable hand-copied manuscripts. Similar resistance was later encountered in much of the Islamic world, where calligraphic traditions were extremely important, and also in the Far East. Despite this resistance, Gutenberg's printing press spread rapidly, and within thirty years of its invention in 1453, towns and cities across Europe had functional printing presses.[1]

As we look just a hundred years beyond the invention of the printing press, we can see how this tool impacted European politics and played a valuable role in inaugurating the Protestant Reformation. The printing press transformed the culture of its era. This is the way epochs always work.

Epochs are generally accompanied by either war or the destruction of those in society who refuse to embrace the values and knowledge that accompany a global epoch. It makes little difference whether the destruction of those who resist epoch reformations takes place intentionally as a result of some militant action or passively as the result of obsolescence, the end result is the same: people and institutions that fail to embrace a global epoch ultimately diminish and then disappear.

The global Internet culture has so profoundly transformed how communication occurs and how relationships form and are maintained that the mediums and structures of today's institutional church seem mundane and antiquated.

Additional examples of global epochs include the telegraph, the telephone, mass transit, radio, television, personal computers and the Internet. Each of these epochs have progressively transformed societal culture. The result? Few people today would consider rewinding the clock to replace the world we now know with that of a previous era.

Christ's church is once again confronting a global epoch. The global Internet culture has so profoundly transformed how communication occurs and how relationships form and are maintained that the mediums and structures that created today's institutional church seem mundane and antiquated. Our institutional churches are at a crossroads, whether we realize it or not. The hard truth is this: we must either embrace the global epoch or die. In much the same way that the traditional churches of the 1940s and '50s were rejected by the television-influenced boomer generation (those born between 1946–1963) as culturally irrelevant, the current global epoch magnifies the discrepancy between relevant and irrelevant immeasurably.

It is in humanity's nature that we filter our understanding of Scripture and worship through our unique cultural distinctives. So while Christians will always share in common the truth of redemption by grace through faith and belief in the divine personhood and all-sufficient work of Jesus Christ, how we implement and apply our understanding of what it means to live for Christ may radically differ from culture to culture. Sadly, many establishment churches and establishment church leaders have become so accustomed to their present cultural paradigm that any means of Christ-centered worship and Christian practice apart from their preferred cultural norm is viewed as strange at best and at worst denounced as theological error. Epochs change culture. Epochs forever change a culture's values and practices. With this in mind, I ask that we proceed through this book with a shared commitment to withhold our judgment against those who are adopting cultural preferences that significantly differ from the establishment.

God foretells global epochs in the book of Daniel (see 2:32–45). He gives Daniel a vision of a great statue divided into various parts, comprised of various materials. Each material element appears to degrade in quality. The head was made of gold, while subsequent body parts were comprised of silver, bronze or iron. The feet of Daniel's statue were made from clay mixed with iron. Theologians have struggled for centuries over how to interpret the iron mixed with clay. However, it is the clay portion of Daniel's statue that is highly relevant to our exploration of the Internet-influenced church. Let's look at just a few differing interpretations:

1. The early-church father Jerome, in his *Commentary on Daniel*,[2] simply ignores this portion of the text and makes no comment.

2. John Calvin interprets the passage to refer to Rome: "They shall be neighbors to others, and that mutual interchange which ought to promote true friendship, shall become utterly profitless. . . . Although they should be mutually united in neighborhood and kindred, yet this would not prevent them from contending with each other with savage enmity, even to the destruction of their empire. Here then the Prophet furnishes us with a vivid picture of the Roman empire, by saying that it was like iron, and also mingled with clay, or mud, as they destroyed themselves by intestine discord after arriving at the highest pitch of fortune."[3]

3. The perspective that iron represents Rome is very common although I believe in error. *The Agora*, a theological website representing a Brethren tradition, advocates that the realms represented in Daniel's statue refer to those nations that would conquer, possess and repress the nation of Israel.[4] *The Agora* presents an intriguing argument with some merit but one that I believe is still somewhat inaccurate.

I could demonstrate scores of variations regarding how honest scholars have tried to make sense of this prophecy. However, in most cases the argument is based upon the statue's two arms, two legs and ten toes. Most common is the perspective that the ten toes represent ten kingdoms that would result from the dissolution of Rome's Western empire. I struggle with this perspective for several reasons:

1. This position represents a theological prejudice that suggests that the nations that emerged from the Western empire were more important than the nations that emerged from the Byzantine Empire in the East (the Byzantine Empire lasted nearly one thousand years longer than the Western empire).

2. This position is built upon the theological construct that the toes (as well as the two arms and two legs) are highly important to the prophetic narrative, a perspective the text does not seem to share with just a mere reference to the toes as being a part of the feet in Daniel 2:41.

3. Verse 45 introduces the "rock cut out of a mountain, but not by human hands" rolling down the mountainside to collide with and destroy all present and previous realms. The beginning of verse 44 is explicit: God's kingdom will be established "in the time of those kings," referencing the period of iron mixed with clay—the period that follows the iron epoch. If the traditional interpretation of the passage is to be accepted, then Christ would have established His kingdom after the iron epoch, not during the iron epoch. History is clear that Christ lived, died and arose from the dead during the Roman period—what this interpretation suggests is the iron epoch. But an additional problem exists: we are told by Daniel as he interprets the dream for us that the rock representing God's kingdom will "crush all those kingdoms and bring them to an end" (2:44). Clearly the destruction of the epochs represented by the feet comprised of iron and baked clay has not yet occurred if the feet truly represent the controversial ten nations that emerged in the West when Roman rule ended.

With these difficulties in mind, I have come to depart from the traditional interpretations of this passage and now believe that each division of Daniel's statue represents an epoch era in humanity's future. At this point we need to wade through a brief Bible history survey to lay a sound foundation for later topics.

The Aramaic word *malchu*, translated as "kingdom," can refer both to a literal kingdom as well as reflect an era of time commonly translated as "realm." The interpretation of "realm" as "a period of time" fits well with our present discussion of "epoch." Certainly the Daniel account begins by listing specific kingdoms, but by the end of the account such distinctions are not so clear. The word "realm" (or, as we could translate it today, "epoch") used in place of "kingdom" appears to fit the overall account most accurately. So Daniel 2:39–45 could just as well be translated this way:

> After you, another [epoch/realm] will arise, inferior to yours. Next, a third [epoch/realm], one of bronze, will rule over the whole earth. Finally, there will be a fourth [epoch/realm], strong as iron—for iron breaks and smashes everything—and as iron breaks things to pieces, so it will crush and break all the others. Just as you saw that the feet and toes were partly of baked clay and partly of iron, so this will be a divided [epoch/realm]; yet it will have some of the strength of iron in it, even as you saw iron mixed with clay. As the toes were partly iron and partly clay, so this [epoch/realm] will be partly strong and partly brittle. And just as you saw the iron mixed with baked clay, so *the people will be a mixture and will not remain united*, any more than iron mixes with clay.
>
> In the time of [the divided epoch/realm], the God of heaven will set up [an epoch/realm] that will never be destroyed, nor will it be left to another people. It will crush all those [epochs/realms] and bring them to an end, but it will itself endure forever. This is the meaning of the vision of the rock cut out of a mountain, but not by human hands—a rock that broke the iron, the bronze, the clay, the silver and the gold to pieces.

I believe that a case can be made for associating the materials depicted in the statue as elements crucial to each epoch era of human history.

The Golden Epoch: Babylon

> The head of the statue was made of pure gold. . . . This was the dream, and now we will interpret it to the king. Your Majesty, you are the king of kings. The God of heaven has given you dominion and power and might and glory; in your hands he has placed all mankind and the beasts of the field and the birds in the sky. Wherever they live, he has made you ruler over them all. You are that head of gold. (Dan. 2:32, 36–38)

It is clear from the text that Daniel identifies the golden head of the statue as representing Babylon. In many ways gold did represent the wealth and power of Babylon. We find in Daniel chapter 3 that King Nebuchadnezzar creates a gold statue of a man ninety feet tall by nine feet wide. Herodotus, the "father of history," also gives us a glimpse into the prestige of the Babylonian Empire in paragraph 183 of his work *Histories*:

> Below, in the same precinct, there is a second temple, in which is a sitting figure of Jupiter, all of gold. Before the figure stands a large golden table, and the throne whereon it sits, and the base on which the throne is placed, are likewise of gold. The Chaldaeans told me that all the gold together was eight hundred talents' weight. Outside the temple are two altars, one of solid gold, on which it is

only lawful to offer sucklings; the other a common altar, but of great size, on which the full-grown animals are sacrificed. It is also on the great altar that the Chaldaeans burn the frankincense, which is offered to the amount of a thousand talents' weight, every year, at the festival of the God. In the time of Cyrus there was likewise in this temple a figure of a man, twelve cubits high, entirely of solid gold.[5]

The Silver Epoch: Medo-Persian Empire

Its chest and arms [were] of silver. . . . After you, another kingdom will arise, inferior to yours. (Dan. 2:32, 39)

Silver was the element that most represented the Medo-Persian Empire, because it was the Medo-Persian Empire that first established standards for weights, measures and currency. These standards permitted national and international trade to take place in a way that had never before been possible. It also permitted the establishment of a banking system that could make loans and collect interest.[6]

King Darius of the Medo-Persian Empire conquered the nation-state of Lydia in 546 BC. This event is important for our discussion regarding epochs, because it was the nation of Lydia that first minted coins to a standardized currency. When Darius conquered Lydia, he encompassed this practice in the Persian economy. His "gold standard" was a coin called the *dareikos*, which could only be minted by the king. The silver version, which could be more broadly minted by governors within the empire, was the dominant currency for use by merchants and traders. It was called a siglos; later the name was more commonly translated "shekels."

All nations from this period on followed the Medo-Persian Empire in this regard—the use of coins as a standard currency was an epoch event in human history.

The Bronze Epoch: Greco-Roman Empire

> Its belly and thighs [were] of bronze. . . . Next, a third kingdom, one of bronze, will rule over the whole earth. (Dan. 2:32, 39)

Historians commonly refer to the two nations of Greece and Rome as one because of how Rome adopted so many of the cultural values and beliefs once held by Greece. One Grecian practice that is of particular interest is the recycling of bronze. Before Rome conquered Greece in 168 BC, Greece had been recycling bronze since 400 BC, especially during times of war or hardship. When Rome defeated Greece, it adopted the art of recycling bronze, but for its own specific military and political purpose: to brand conquered nations as a part of the Roman Empire. The American University in Washington DC explains in one of their online learning TED (Technology, Entertainment and Design) case studies,

> In ancient times, Roman dominance became pervasive throughout the Mediterranean world. In the process, they sought to supplant ancient religions and political systems

in the conquered regions with their own methods. Thus, worn metal statues commemorating ancient gods or heroes, which had stood for ages in the public areas in the cities of the conquered regions, were torn down and sent to Rome. This scrap metal was melted down and recast as either weapons for the Roman legions or new statues which were dedicated to historic Roman events or leaders.[7]

The *Palimpsest This!* website expands upon this line of thought based upon the writings of Pliny the Elder:

> One can argue that this ancient bronze recycling trade was founded primarily on political reasons rather than economical ones. As the Roman Empire expanded throughout the Mediterranean world, the areas under Roman control needed to be secured using a psychological tactic—the statues of idols that the conquered people had been attached to would be removed from all the public squares and agoras.[8]

According to David Noy of the University of Wales, it was this very practice of erecting Roman statues in conquered territories that caused the people of Israel to incite rebellion against Rome:

> In 39 or 40 c.e., the Emperor Gaius Caligula decided to have a statue of himself installed in the Jewish Temple at Jerusalem. He ordered the governor of Syria, Petronius, to use as much military force as necessary to erect it. Petronius was confronted with thousands of protesting Judean Jews before he had even left Syria, and procrastinated as

long as possible. Jews throughout the Roman world were horrified at the greatest threat to the monotheistic and aniconic nature of their worship for 200 years: the statue was to them "a sight unfit to see" (Philo, *Leg.* 224), and they were appalled.[9]

Lastly, we must remember that the Daniel text itself describes this epoch as ruling over "the whole earth" (2:35). Certainly the Greco-Roman Empire encompassed more people than any other previous kingdom. But even more importantly, the influence of the Greco-Roman Empire can still be felt and observed today in Western cultures and beyond through republican political structures, art, architecture and language.

The Iron Epoch: Industrial Revolution

> Its legs [were] of iron. . . . Finally, there will be a fourth kingdom, strong as iron—for iron breaks and smashes everything—and as iron breaks things to pieces, so it will crush and break all the others. (Dan. 2:33, 40)

The iron epoch is unlike any of the previous epochs. In fact, Daniel states, "It will crush and break all others," referring, of course, to the previous epoch realms. When we consider the geography of the previous epoch realms, to a large extent each realm built upon much the same territory as its predecessors—especially in and around the geography of Judah and Israel. This new iron element, we are told, would destroy the geographical and historical foundations held in common by the previous epoch eras and so become an epoch era unlike any that had ever existed before. I believe that the iron in Daniel's statue addresses the Industrial Revolution, which was built upon iron along with the steel that purified iron produces. The means of industry and manufacturing almost always requires iron and steel machines to be invented and implemented. Without the use of iron and steel, there would be little industry possible. Iron is essential to this epoch era.

The Industrial Revolution had its roots in the Enlightenment, a period also known as the Age of Reason. From this period on, intellectual development, creativity and industry would evolve as the world had never before experienced. Joseph A. Montagna of the Yale–New Haven Teachers Institute remarks,

> The era known as the Industrial Revolution was a period in which fundamental changes occurred in agriculture, textile and metal manufacture, transportation, economic policies and the social structure. . . . This period is appropriately labeled "revolution," for it thoroughly *destroyed the old manner of doing things* [per Dan. 2:40]; yet the term is simultaneously inappropriate, for it connotes abrupt change. The changes that occurred during this period (1760–1850), in fact, occurred gradually. The year 1760 is generally accepted as the "eve" of the Industrial Revolution. In reality, this eve began more than two centuries before this date. The late 18th century and the early 19th century brought to fruition the ideas and discoveries of those who had long passed on, such as, Galileo, Bacon, Descartes and others.[10]

The Industrial Revolution truly had no geographical boundaries. It quickly spread throughout Western Europe and into North America. And in many ways it is still expanding into third world countries that provide inexpensive means of manufacturing. This is a very important point to emphasize, for in the last epoch era represented in Daniel's statue, there will be a continuation of the previous epoch era—the iron that comprised the legs also defines culture in the feet. As Daniel moves beyond the iron era in his interpretation of the king's dream, we see another epoch era introduced and blended into the human timeline that does not supplant the previous epoch era. This is the only time in human history that two epoch eras will coexist, but they will coexist with stress and disunity.

The Iron and Clay Epochs: Industrial Revolution and Information Revolution

Its feet [were] partly of iron and partly of *baked clay*. . . . Just as you saw that the feet and toes were partly of *baked clay* and partly of iron, so this will be a divided kingdom; yet it will have some of the strength of iron in it, even as you saw iron mixed with clay. As the toes were partly iron and partly clay, so this kingdom will be partly strong and *partly brittle*. And just as you saw the iron mixed with *baked clay*, so the people will be a mixture and will not remain united, any more than iron mixes with clay. (Dan. 2:33, 41–43)

The iron/clay feet have always mystified theologians, first because clay is not a metal and second because human society seems to be improving over time rather than corrupting as the baser materials in the statue would suggest. However, only within the past fifty years has it finally been possible to truly identify the clay among the epochs of human history.

The era of baked clay began in 1947. In this same year in which the United Nations voted to partition Israel and Palestine, thereby reestablishing the nation of Israel—a major prophetic marker in Scripture—the first transistor was invented. Then, in the 1950s, silicon quickly replaced germanium as the preferred material used within transistorized components because it was more stable under heat than germanium. Silicon is the second-most common element on planet Earth, second only to oxygen—it is the sand that comprises our planet.

Our present world runs on baked chacaph, *just as was prophesied by Daniel. Every computer, every electronic device that processes information is built upon silicon* (chacaph).

Silicon is the foundational element for clay. In its baked form in Daniel's time clay was used to make pottery. However, more specifically, a *chacaph* (rendered as "clay" in the book of Daniel) is generally considered a broken shard; in its verb form the word means "to flake off." Three times

Daniel 2 makes clear that the clay being referenced in the account of the statue is not miry clay but rather clay that is baked and brittle (see 2:33, 41, 43). It is this material that Daniel references and that depicts the final epoch of humanity's future—the epoch that is blended into the already-established iron epoch.

Today we use "baked flakes," or brittle wafers of *chacaph*, in every transistor and integrated circuit used in modern electronic equipment. Creating these baked silicon wafers begins with growing silicon crystal "staffs," which are baked to over 1,500 degrees Fahrenheit and then sawed into very thin wafers. These wafers are extremely thin and brittle. The edge of the wafer is then rounded using a fine diamond cutter; this process is necessary to keep the brittle edges of the silicon wafer from "flaking off."[11] (Note that *chacaph*, "flaking off," is the exact wording used within the document cited).

Our present world runs on baked *chacaph*, just as was prophesied by Daniel. Every computer, every electronic device that processes information is built upon silicon (*chacaph*). We live in the clay epoch, an era of technological information and communication. Silicon transistors gave birth to the digital age, which made computers and the Internet possible. In this era the way that people connect, relate and share information is rapidly transforming. The iron epoch, the Industrial Age, is waning but still very much a part of global cultures. The apex of this era was the vacuum-tube powered television culture—a culture that concluded in the late 1980s.

The clay epoch is not just emerging—it is now present. Unfortunately, so many churches today still identify better with the values of the established industrial iron epoch than they do with the values of the clay epoch. The ultimate goal of this book is to help the church make the transition from established iron-epoch cultural values to respecting the values and culture that are present and yet emerging within the clay epoch. Daniel warns that brittle clay and iron will be mixed ineffectively in the last epoch of human history. And so some nations, institutions and people still embrace the iron epoch, while many other people and institutions, particularly within first world countries, now embrace the clay epoch. Daniel 2:43 states, "*So the people will be a mixture and will not remain united.*" Christ's church also reflects the disparate cultural values of iron and clay. We are a culturally mixed people as far as our attachments to these epoch eras are concerned. We are not united. And to a certain extent, cultural disparity among our churches is understandable, for the church can and must minister effectively to people within both cultural epochs. Unfortunately, it seems far easier for Christ's church to retreat into previous epoch realms than to confront and invade an emerging one. Church methodologies and practices of the past have created a well-worn and obvious path for church leaders, whereas the emerging epoch remains largely uncharted territory.

It is my intent to introduce this uncharted territory. Although we will evaluate the Internet culture in consider-
e detail, it is not so much with the goal of challenging

churches to go online to form an e-church. Nor will we exclusively evaluate today's millennial generation and its distinct characteristics, comprised of those born between the early 1980s and early 2000s, although we will discuss the millennial generation as pioneers who first advanced the current global epoch. Trends such as e-churches and others associated with the millennial generation come and go and may not be applicable even in a few short years.

Rather, church leaders would do better to focus upon the emerging cultural values shared by people of the clay epoch, values that will likely impact how we will "do church" for generations to come. Epochs are like that. They do not simply impact the generation in which they occur. Epochs forever transform global culture. The sun is now setting on the boomer generation's vision of ministry, a vision that promoted an attraction-presentational methodology, influenced by and modeled upon the medium of television. Today a new and uniquely relational, interactive ministry culture is taking shape. This form of ministry culture will make the completion of the Great Commission even more attainable. The clay epoch enables us as never before to go into all the world and make disciples. But the transition to this epoch will be difficult for those who cling to iron-epoch values.

The tensions that exist between those who hold to an iron-era ministry philosophy, epitomized by a television-influenced values set, as compared to those who hold a ministry philosophy born of the Internet-influenced era, are profound. These tensions, if left unaddressed, threaten to impede the incredible kingdom-impact potential of an Internet-influenced church.

1

Tension in the Internet Era

We believe that understanding and resolving the tensions arising from perceptions about the net generation *can only be achieved if we use a lens that considers technology, values, and behavior as a closely coupled triad of factors affecting the perceived organizational tensions.*

Karine Nahon, "Executives: Don't Try to Change the Net Generation"

I must begin this book by asserting that, for the most part, the boomer generation does not appreciate what the Internet culture has become. The advent of the Internet has been received by many boomers as an intrusion into a lifestyle that was firmly established before the Internet ever became a reality. Although the Internet was invented by boomers, the subsequent Gen X generation, born between the early 1960s and the early '80s, helped it move beyond mere static websites and e-mail and to morph into an interactive and relational environment.

29

Daniel 2:41 describes the final human epoch as a "divided" world distinguished by two kinds of people groups: those who prefer the iron epoch and those who prefer the clay epoch. I believe that this tension began to reveal itself when personal computers and the Internet became commonplace.

By most accounts the Internet as we presently perceive it was birthed around 1991 but did not become truly usable by the average person until Microsoft launched Windows 95 on August 24, 1995, with its integrated Internet browser and e-mail client. So at the writing of this book, most people have only experienced the Internet for less than seventeen years. For the boomer generation, this means that they previously experienced at least twenty-nine years of their lives—these years being their formative ones in which they were most open to exploration and change—without the Internet. By the time the Internet became a reality, the boomer generation was very set in its ways and values.

Even though some within the boomer generation have since adapted to many aspects of the Web 2.0+ generation of the Internet (the user-interactive Internet that allows people to network with each other through social media, blogs and the like), the primary difference between boomers and millennials (those following Gen X) in this regard is that boomers perceive the Internet as a tool to be taken up and put down as necessary, whereas millennials view the Internet as an integrated way of life. They cannot imagine life without the Internet. Millennials are, after all, the first generation to be unaware of what the world was like without the Internet. This important distinction cannot be over-emphasized. Let's look at a few comparative generalizations regarding each generation. Again, there may be exceptions to the norms, but in general the following is accurate:

Millennials — *Internet Natives*	Boomers — *Internet Immigrants*
Texting: Text constantly to keep in touch with friends and to keep up on events.	**Texting:** Rarely text, but when they do, it is usually to communicate with a daughter or son.
Facebook: Check Facebook every day to keep current with friends or to update their profile with a new post.	**Facebook:** Likely not to have a Facebook account unless it is to "friend" their children in order to "stalk" them for negative or dangerous behaviors or to post family pictures.
Skype/Facetime: Use video conferencing programs to interact with friends and collaborate on projects.	**Skype/Facetime:** Generally do not use at all unless to keep in touch with children away from home.

In a world in which 64 percent of "wired" Americans have used the Internet for spiritual and religious purposes,[1] the body of Christ must learn to understand and appreciate the emerging Internet-inspired culture. Failure to do so relegates our churches to irrelevancy.

I love the ironic words of Douglas Adams, creator of *The Hitchhiker's Guide to the Galaxy*, regarding generational adoption of new technology. I present this quote in detail for full impact:

I suppose earlier generations had to sit through all this huffing and puffing with the invention of television, the phone, cinema, radio, the car, the bicycle, printing, the wheel and so on, but you would think we would learn the way these things work, which is this: 1) Everything that's already in the world when you're born is just normal; 2) Anything that gets invented between then and before you turn thirty is incredibly exciting and creative and with any luck you can make a career out of it; 3) Anything that gets invented after you're thirty is against the natural order of things and the beginning of the end of civilization as we know it until it's been around for about ten years when it gradually turns out to be alright really.[2]

Adams then continues to explain that these new technologies inspire humanity to transform language. For example, "interactivity" was a social dynamic very normal and commonplace for historic societies before our technological revolution but was largely lost in twentieth century social structures. In the twentieth century we listened passively to the radio, we passively watched television, we passively went to the movies, and we passively attended church. Certainly we did these things with other people in the room, but there was little relational interactivity taking place during these events. Douglas Adams continues his discussion along this vein by providing a fictitious dialogue between a teacher and student:

I expect that history will show "normal" mainstream twentieth century media to be the aberration in all this. "Please, miss, you mean they could only just sit there and watch? They couldn't *do* anything? Didn't everybody feel terribly isolated or alienated or ignored?" "Yes, child, that's why they all went mad. Before the Restoration." "What was the Restoration again, please, miss?" "The end of the twentieth century, child. When we started to get interactivity back."[3]

Marc Prenskey is accredited with being the first person to coin the terms "digital natives" and "digital immigrants."[4] I wish to expand upon his labels as they apply to and impact the local church by also identifying the various Internet generations as *foreigners, immigrants* and *natives*.

Internet Foreigners

The *foreigner* has lived most of his or her life without computers or the Internet. For those in this generation, computers and the Internet are commonly viewed as a cultural intrusion. They tend to fear technology because they do not understand it. Sadly , however, this category of people, mostly those age sixty-five and older, generally hold positions of influence within our church boards and often still serve as senior pastors. These decision makers typically cannot relate to the Internet culture. This generation will spend millions of dollars to build large worship centers and scores of thousands of dollars annually to support traditional missionaries, all of which may reach a mere few thousand people each year. This is their culture. Buildings and missionaries are tangible things that they can see and touch.

This builder generation, which preceded that of the boomers, is also known as the radio generation. In their formative years, during the 1920s and '30s, radio was the primary "high-tech" communication medium. The radio culture reinforced a passive auditory learning preference resulting in the promotion of the monologue sermon within the local church. This generation harnessed their radio technology to extend the monologue gospel message throughout the world using regional and shortwave radio broadcasts.

Internet Immigrants

Many *immigrants* have lived over half their lives without computers or the Internet yet in recent years have been forced to make a drastic transition into a new technical world. These individuals are also called the television generation.[5] This generation perceives using technology as sitting passively while watching a favorite television show, all the while being bombarded with repetitious advertisements. These experiences have shaped a culture in which people possess marketing savvy and value how things look.

The advent of the Willow Creek church model in the 1980s fit perfectly with boomer television values. The Willow Creek ministry model emphasized the need to understand the unchurched "Harry" and "Mary"[6] within a community. Church leaders were encouraged to canvas their communities to discover the issues that kept people from attending church and then to structure the Sunday morning programming (note the use of "programming," a television production term) to address these seeker-targeted issues (note the use of "targeting," another term often used in television marketing).

In churches that have adopted this model, the majority of financial, human and time resources are invested into the production of the Sunday morning program. The concept of a contemporary church is, to a large extent, a theme-based program that people passively observe. The program, this philosophy asserts, must fit within the time-framework of a one-hour television show and no longer than a short movie (ninety minutes). In spite of all the energy and resources invested into these complex and targeted programs, within a few weeks of viewing them, attendees can often recall very little of what was taught in the topical message, what songs they sang or who they spoke with in the church lobby.

The television culture that many Internet immigrants were born into transformed learning preferences from auditory (from the radio-era influence of the Internet foreigner's generation) to visual. However, in a television culture we are so bombarded with imagery that unless the images are often repeated (via reruns, commercials, etc.), mentally rehearsed and applied in one's life, the concepts being communicated are not generally retained in the long-term memory.[7]

Internet Natives

While passive learning is a defining value for Internet foreigners (generally the builder generation) and Internet immigrants (generally the boomer generation), this is not a word that can be used to describe the *native* culture. The native culture is defined by a preference for interactive multisensory experiences. This culture has been shaped by computer-based video games as well as interactive Internet-based multimedia and social networking. Natives are accustomed to touching their iPad screen or using a computer mouse to click on a button and receive an immediate gratifying response.

Natives want to interact with their environment and through that interaction to have a measure of influence over environmental outcomes. In fact, a 2005 CBS focus-group study reported by the *60 Minutes* television show polled millennials regarding their cultural preferences. One hundred percent of the focus-group participants expressed that they would rather use the Internet than watch television.[8] Those in the focus group stated that their primary reason for this preference was that they were unable to control what happens within a television show. Acknowledging these cultural preferences, the television industry now offers reality shows such as *American Idol* in which young adults can text message their votes and thereby "influence" the results of the show. These themes, "interactivity" and "influencing outcomes," severely challenge the values of our television-influenced church models that promote passive observation over personal interactivity and hierarchical corporate leadership over grassroots personal influence.

Internet natives are young adults who have never known life without computers or the Internet. Their age spectrum is generally defined as approximately fifteen to thirty-two years of age and comprises nearly 30 percent of the population, according to U.S. census projections. Yet with each succeeding year, this culture expands. Within the next ten to fifteen years, the native culture will be the dominant people-category within the Christian community. As a category, this group is sometimes referred to as millennials or echo boomers. The concept of an echo is that sound has bounced off from an object and reversed direction so that a person can hear the results. Similarly, the echo boomer's culture has reversed direction from that of previous generations. To a great extent the values of the builder and boomer generations and to a lesser extent the Gen X generations are rejected by echo boomers/millennials as shallow and non-relational. Interestingly enough, the boomer generation in particular tends to make this same accusation of the echo boomers. In the end, such labels simply are not helpful if our goal is to bridge the cultural epochs and minister to both the people of the iron realm as well as the people of the clay realm.

It is common today to find books that address the post-modern and/or emergent church. Most of these books focus upon the theological impact that the emerging culture has had upon how a church communicates its message. Sadly, some of these voices have lost their influence within Christ's church due to doctrinal apostasy. Yet there are many other similar prophets who have rightly challenged the church to take a fresh look at itself, its strategies and its methodologies so that it might remain relevant to an ever-transforming culture. There is much that the church can learn regarding how we do church. Yet ministry relevancy is only possible when those who serve in Christ's name faithfully honor our Lord and Master Jesus Christ by staying true to His nature in the manner by which we serve *and* true to His clear, uncompromising and exclusive gospel message. To do any less is to make "relevancy" an idol that we set before God and our Savior Jesus Christ.

In years past cultural transformations occurred generation by generation. A generation was considered to comprise approximately thirty years.[9] Today, however, cultural transformations occur often within a span of three to five years. There was a time when the church was a driver and definer of society and culture, and yet today the local church often finds itself trying to keep up culturally with the 1980s.

Clearly, iron-epoch and clay-epoch biblically based ministries are both about making disciples of Jesus Christ. Regardless of the era, modern or postmodern, we all understand that disciple making is best accomplished through authentic relationships and biblically sound teaching. At the core of effective disciple making is an authentic relational process by which the disciple seeks to pattern his or her life after a teacher. But how this process occurs is where the agreement between people of the iron epoch and those of the clay epoch diverge.

People of the iron-epoch culture perceive that relationships are forged and maintained in church lobbies, living rooms and small groups, through common employment or over coffee. At the same time, communication in this culture has been largely influenced by the monologue mediums of radio and television. Television and radio are media that are relationally passive and interactionally challenged.

Therefore, people of the iron epoch perceive relational interaction as only truly possible when people meet together in a common place and at a common time. Although the telephone may contradict this cultural bias at some level, people of the iron epoch generally consider telephone communication as an inferior substitute to their interpersonal ideal. People of this era often emphasize the need to be present with a person because so much of the communication process, they assert, occurs though observation of empathic nonverbals.

People of the clay-epoch culture do not dismiss the relational values espoused by those of the iron epoch, they simply add layers to it: additional mediums such as cell phones, social media, instant messaging, video conferencing, texting and so on that serve to enhance relational connections.

People of the iron-epoch culture typically criticize young adults of the clay-epoch culture as anti-relational people who would rather sit in front of a computer screen than sit face to face with people. Similarly, people of the clay-epoch culture criticize the iron-epoch culture as anti-relational, because if relationships were really important to them, they ask, then why do they wait weeks or months to connect socially? The iron-epoch culture and the clay-epoch culture are like the proverbial "two ships passing in the night," both sharing the same values but implementing those values differently. As one young adult shared with me, "I cannot imagine what life would be like if I could not be in constant connection with my friends."[10] The importance of authentic relationships among the people of the

clay realm cannot be overstated. Lack of value for such relationships is one of the major criticisms they assert against
the establishment church. The criticism reveals itself most
profoundly in the failure of the iron-epoch church to effectively make disciples of Jesus Christ.[11]

To a large extent, today's iron-epoch ministry strategies
are failing to effectively make disciples. This is due in part to
our church paradigms being generally attractional-presentational, influenced largely by television-inspired values, that
emphasize how Christianity "looks" rather than modeling
an authentic Christian life. The clay-epoch culture tends
to reject presentational imagery in favor of relational and
spiritual authenticity and interactivity. One young blogger
shared his perspective regarding the iron-epoch paradigm
of Christianity with the world:

> I quit being a Christian. I'll never quit following Christ,
> and living a life that he has called me to. But I quit be-
> ing a Christian. I want to be able to proclaim to people
> when I'm having a hard time. I want to be honest with
> people and let them know it's been a month since I've
> done my devotions. That's what real Christianity is. It's
> not the peaches and cream we ascribe it to be. It's not
> about being perfect. It's about doing the best we can,
> despite our imperfections. Sometimes I don't feel like
> being a Christian anymore. It doesn't mean I'm not, just
> because I have that feeling. Sometimes I have to question
> my entire belief system, including the existence of God
> himself. That doesn't mean I'm not a Christian. I have
> doubts. I have questions. Sometimes I just don't feel like

doing it. That doesn't make me any less of a Christian. No, the fact that I am open and honest about those things to me means that if anything, my relationship with God is just that much truer. No human relationship that's worth anything is all about being perfect. My friends and I share all our emotions—the times when we feel great, and the times when we feel crappy. Telling God that I'm doubting something about my faith doesn't mean he doesn't love me anymore, praise Him! . . . So, it is with virulent disdain I say goodbye to Christianity. I'm not about pretending anymore. Out with Christianity! In with a true, honest, relationship with Jesus Christ—and the people he loved so much, he died for them.[12]

Unfortunately, this blogger is not alone in his rejection of the iron-epoch model of Christianity that emphasizes image over relational and spiritual substance. If this blogger represented an isolated case, then there would be no need for this book. David Kinnaman, president of the Barna Group, a cultural research group, summarized his findings regarding how young Christians and non-Christians alike are now distancing themselves from the iron-feet culture's definition of Christianity. Kinnaman explained,

That's where the term 'unChristian' came from. Young people are very candid. In our interviews, we kept encountering young people—both those inside the church and outside of it—who said that something was broken in the present-day expression of Christianity. Their perceptions about Christianity were not always accurate, but what surprised me was not only the severity of their frustration with Christians, but also how frequently young born again Christians expressed some of the very same comments as young non-Christians.[13]

It is not simply the average young follower of Christ who has come to reject the iron-realm paradigm of church and Christianity. Some church leaders, even those who have only known iron-realm cultural values, are beginning to honestly reflect upon the true cost of what they have invested so much time, energy and resources to build. Some time ago I was contacted by a church whose senior pastor had once served a mega-ministry designed by iron-realm people for iron-realm people. However, this pastor had now rejected the iron-realm model and sought to develop a more authentic relational ministry. This church wanted to extend their relational ministry efforts online through a web ministry that targeted the hurts and issues that people had experienced due to the iron-realm church paradigm. Their web ministry home page began with these words:

> An open letter to the world: As Christians, we ask your forgiveness for being self-righteous and arrogant. We have all too often packaged our faith into an unworkable formula and then criticized and demeaned people who could not make the formula work. Formula-Christianity is not a safe faith. It hurts people by disillusioning their faith in Christ. At its core it is a lie. It promises us an easy spiritual journey, and yet its road is replete with dangerous sinkholes.[14]

At a leadership conference I found myself speaking to a young woman who, just like the first blogger I mentioned, was uncomfortable calling herself a Christian. Her issue was not that she did not believe in Jesus Christ as God's Son and as her Savior but that she no longer believed in the local church. She was confused about her spiritual identity because she had come to devalue what the local church presented to her as Christianity. I will never forget her words to me regarding her perception of the television-influenced church—they cut me to the core: "It does not take a real Christian to put on a Christian show; I am looking for something that is more real."

People who comprise the Internet-influenced church are typically not interested in a plasticized Barbie-and-Ken Christianity. They know better.

So here's the truth: the biblical message communicated through the church is not the problem. The message is true. The message is unchanging. The message is the "good news" that the world desperately needs. However, the message has now become lost in our medium-influenced methodology. By overlaying a television-culture paradigm onto the church, a paradigm that values how things look and passive observation, we have made the message appear too packaged—too plastic. People who comprise the Internet-influenced church are typically not interested in a plasticized Barbie-and-Ken Christianity. They know better. When people of the Internet culture receive messages that sound too good to be true in their e-mail inbox, they immediately mark the message as spam and move the message to their virtual trash can. In the minds and hearts of many young adults today, they are labeling the message of the television-influenced church as "spam" and moving the message into their spiritual trash can. The more they are confronted with such spam, the more ardently they resist the message.

So how can an iron-epoch model church and its iron-epoch leaders, who for years have only known the television culture, begin to transform itself into an Internet-influenced church? Earlier I mentioned the iron-era church's effort to understand the needs of unbelievers, a principle that came from Lee Strobel's book *Inside the Mind of Unchurched Harry and Mary*, which taught the church how to become sensitive to the needs and values of its generation. Lee's principles are still valid. We begin by first reorienting our ministries to focus upon their Christ-ordained mission directives and then relearn how to accomplish our mission directives in a manner that is appropriate to the needs and values of the Internet-influenced culture.

2

Navigating a Paradigm Shift

---

*Your paradigm is so intrinsic to your mental process
that you are hardly aware of its existence, until you try to
communicate with someone with a different paradigm.*

Donella Meadows, *The Global Citizen*

Paradigms are human-generated constructs consisting
of personal perspectives and functional systems that
help us interact with our world. We have all been
influenced by paradigms and have knowingly, or at times
unwittingly, integrated them into our lives. A paradigm can
be as mundane as a cultural choice such as whether to eat
using chopsticks or a fork. It can also be as foundationally
critical as the ministry strategies in which we choose to
invest our time, finances and human resources. Paradigms
give us a false belief that we can understand the world
around us and therefore better manage and interact with
that world. I say "a false belief" because paradigms are

constantly changing. For this reason a wise leader does not hold firmly to established paradigms. A wise leader anticipates paradigm shifts and prepares his or her followers for the emotional, psychological and practical transitions required to accommodate emerging paradigms.

A number of years ago, a large corporation based in Holland, Michigan, developed a leadership training program. As part of this program, they addressed "personal paradigms" in an effort to get their leaders to think out of the box. To this end they showed a short movie (no longer in production) that featured bicycle seats to illustrate the principle they wanted to convey. As the account goes, a manufacturer had devised a new kind of seat that eliminated all the discomfort commonly associated with the "saddle paradigm." However, because the seat looked entirely unlike people's perception of what a bike seat should look like, the new product, although far superior to the traditional one, failed to succeed in the bike market.

Holding firm to the paradigms of the past and working harder to implement them will never advance Christ's kingdom in this ever-changing world.

Donella Meadows, in her quote at the start of this chapter, was right. We are often unaware of the perceptual paradigms we have integrated into our lives and ministries. And rarely do we assess them. Rarely do we ask ourselves if our ministry paradigms are still valid or whether they are truly effective. Humanity's natural response to an obsolete paradigm is not to change the paradigm but to work harder to prove the antiquated paradigm still valid.

Years ago I served as a pastor within a mainstream denomination. Each year churches within that denomination submitted a statistical report for the official records. One of the items in the report was the number of conversions that had taken place in the church in that year. I was stunned to see church after church reporting less than three conversions in the previous year, a statistic consistently outperformed by the numbers of reported deaths. Many churches within that denomination listed no conversions within a single year! Clearly, if our goal was to expand Christ's kingdom in this world, our established paradigm for doing church was no longer working. So how did the denominational leadership respond? Their solution was to "go back to Egypt!" The leaders challenged their churches to do church the way it had been done in the 1940s and '50s. They simply wanted to work harder in an attempt to prove an antiquated paradigm still valid. This was not the most effective move.

Global epochs force us to confront our established paradigms. Established ministry systems that have worked well in the past must now adapt to the present epoch's influence. Holding firm to the paradigms of the past and working harder to implement them will never advance Christ's kingdom in this ever-changing world.

I have already asserted numerous times that a distinction must be made between churches that are influenced by a television culture and churches influenced by the Internet culture. The two cultures do not coexist well. In fact, their values and their application of those values are quite distinct from one another.

The influence of the television culture upon society at large and the church in America specifically first hit home for me in 1987 when I read Neil Postman's groundbreaking book *Amusing Ourselves to Death*.

Postman, a professor of communication at New York University, wrote his book in 1984 at the height of the television era. The year is significant for another reason in that Postman's book responded in part to George Orwell's *1984* vision of the future. Orwell depicted a future in which government would use technology to impose its will upon every facet of society. While this perspective may have been true for some nations in the actual year of 1984, it was not a vision that best described American society at that time. Rather, Postman developed a profound argument favoring the view of Aldous Huxley in his book *Brave New World*. Huxley proposed that technology would create a society in which pleasure would lull humanity into an intellectual and political slumber. Postman perceived that technology was indeed doing this very thing! It was creating just such a passive society.

Granted, Postman's intention was to redirect society away from television and back to the written word. However, he did live to see the birth of the Internet and its early transformative effects upon society. He died in 2003 while the Internet was still in its pre-2.0 stage of evolution, its content primarily static. Many of the principles that Postman espoused are still valid in our present discourse regarding paradigm shifts. In *Amusing Ourselves to Death*, he lays out his thesis:

> To say it, then, as plainly as I can, this book is an inquiry into and a lamentation about the most significant American cultural fact of the second half of the twentieth century: the decline of the Age of Typography and the ascendancy of the Age of Television. This changeover has dramatically and irreversibly shifted the content and meaning of public discourse, since *two media so vastly different cannot accommodate the same ideas.* As the influence of print wanes, the content of politics, religion, education, and anything else that comprises public business must change and be recast in terms that are most suitable to television.[1]

An additional and unintentional reason that the period surrounding 1984 was a profound time for Postman's writings was that in 1981 a rather new congregation called *Willow Creek* moved into their new campus facilities in Barrington, Illinois. Within a few years the "Willow Creek model" was born. This model patterned itself after attractional-presentational television values. The Willow Creek staff studied their community's Harrys and Marys, all of whom had been raised within a television culture. The information gleaned from these studies resulted in a church service designed to be highly programmed, directed and presented. Soon this model was replicated within many churches around the country. This only made sense at the time, since by framing the gospel message within the television-influenced cultural context, the church's audience would best understand and receive the message. By 1992 the Willow Creek Society launched online to interlink churches that shared the ministry philosophy espoused by Willow Creek. Their philosophy espoused a television-influenced methodology that in general included the following elements:

- *Attractional ministry.* Services were culturally sensitive, "seeker sensitive" and designed to enable attendees to bring nonchurched friends to observe Willow Creek presentations.

- *Professional programming.* Services were planned and produced down to fifteen-second increments and used a "stage director" to oversee the production.

- *Projection screens and video.* The "production" was made larger than life by projecting video of stage members as well as song lyrics onto large screens to help keep the audience's focus on the stage.

- *Market-targeted topical messaging.* All communication media, whether onstage, onscreen or in print, targeted the felt needs of spiritual "seekers."

- *Interest-oriented programs.* The church provided many television-like "channels" based upon the needs/desires of their consumers such as women's ministry, men's ministry, children's ministry, youth ministry, singles' ministry and others.

- *Planting of churches in theaters.* For the Willow Creek model, the "church world is all a stage," and the audience's attention was to be focused upon what happens onstage. This made theater facilities ideal models for Willow Creek church plants.

---

*Two media so vastly different
cannot accommodate the same ideas.*

Before you think I am being too harsh, I must confess that prior to the ascendancy of the Internet, I was a devotee of the Willow Creek model. I used the model when starting and revitalizing churches. I used the *Promiseland* children's ministry curriculum, which was modeled after the adult-church strategies, before the curriculum was even formally published! The Willow Creek model succeeded at attracting many attendees; but over time it became evident to me, as well as to many other pastors, that presentational church was a poor strategy for disciple making (see, for example, Willow Creek's *Reveal* study).

When the Internet was born and its influence upon the television-inspired culture unfolded, it soon became evident that Neil Postman's words of warning were true: "Two media so vastly different cannot accommodate the same ideas." Today pastors promote their television values online through streamed video of their sermons and/or services as if the Internet was just another television distribution system. The result is that fewer and fewer clay-epoch

Christians continue to attend the establishment church. Many churches have found it difficult to attract and keep people under the age of twenty-nine. The Southern Baptist Convention, one of the largest Protestant denominations in the world, has studied their churches and have found that 88 percent of young people who have been raised within an evangelical church leave the church at age eighteen and never return.[2] Neil Postman warns us of this transition in cultural values:

> Whatever the original and limited context of its use may have been, a medium has the power to fly far beyond that context. . . . Because of the way it directs us to organize our minds and integrate our experience of the world, it imposes itself on our consciousness and social institutions in myriad forms. It sometimes has the power to become implicated in our concepts of piety . . . and it is always implicated in the ways we define and regulate our ideas of truth.[3]

The epistemology of the television culture and the epistemology of the Internet culture are contrary to one another. How the two cultures learn, share and acquire knowledge as well as relate to others and find meaning in life is vastly different.

Postman continues later in the book,

> They delude themselves who believe that television and [Internet] coexist, for coexistence implies parity. There is no parity here. [Television] is now a residual

epistemology, and it will remain so, aided to some extent by the computer . . . made to look like television screens.[4]

The paradigm has now shifted. The television and the Internet are two epistemologies that cannot coexist (epistemology is the philosophic study of how humanity learns and acquires knowledge). There is no parity between the epistemology of these two influences on culture. They are contrary to one another. How the two cultures learn, share and acquire knowledge as well as relate to others and find meaning in life is vastly different. If you doubt, simply ask an older middle-aged person and a child or young adult which they prefer: watching television or surfing the Internet. It's likely that the young person will prefer the Internet while the older middle-aged person will prefer television. My son Joshua is a clear illustration of this point. He will spend hours on the Internet, and even when we try to watch a family movie, he will begrudgingly join us in our entertainment room but bring his iPad with him so he can multitask.

The people of the iron-epoch culture generally value media solely for its entertainment value. Radio, television and movies exist to provide passive amusement. While this culture will be quick to emphasize that these mediums may also educate, relatively few boomers buy or rent documentaries or watch PBS programming. And in all cases, the epistemology of the television culture is almost exclusively a passive monologue: those of this culture tend to sit together in classrooms and large auditoriums and listen passively to lectures or sermons just as they sit together passively to watch a movie or a television program. This indeed is a strange form of togetherness. Very little interaction and dialogue takes place in this culture's means of acquiring knowledge. Transferring knowledge in this culture tends to occur within a corporate-hierarchical institutional construct in which the school, the church or the television/movie studio will present the information it wishes to share packaged in a manner that it has predetermined. In this way a monologue media format edits truth and often conveys an information prejudice. Dissident voices and ideas are not conveyed or appreciated when offered to this culture's knowledge editors.

This top-down knowledge flow is entirely foreign to the Internet-influenced culture. The epistemology of this group is largely shaped by the information they themselves choose to acquire and digest.

This kind of top-down knowledge flow is entirely foreign to the Internet-influenced culture. The epistemology of this group is largely shaped by the information they themselves choose to acquire and digest. Information acquired is shared and tested via the global "conversation" on any and all topics of value to humanity within the Internet. This conversation is truly a global dialogue in which each person within the clay-epoch culture may contribute his or her personal perspectives and biases. The challenge for the church today, if it is not already clear, is that the global voices who decry Christ and His church far outweigh the global voices for Christ and His church. Christ's church needs to get more engaged in the conversation if it ever hopes to compete.

Conversation in an Internet-influenced culture, however, often morphs into interactive collaboration. My daughter is a sophomore in a local public high school. Every student in her school was issued their own personal Apple iPad 2. Most of the learning projects assigned by my daughter's teachers require group participation. So to accomplish their project goals, study groups meet together virtually using Skype to video conference with each other. The Internet provides my daughter and her team an abundance of information as well as the means to work together to process that information. This grassroots epistemological experience is normative for the people of the clay-epoch culture yet quite abnormal for the people of the iron-epoch culture.

Collaborative interaction as a discipleship paradigm is antithetical to methodology practiced by most iron-epoch pastors. We pastors like to look like the professionals. We like to have our teachings prepared with excellence. We are, by the way, the knowledgeable authority figures who graduated from seminary. And if some of us were really honest, we'd admit that we like to hear ourselves talk. Finally, we consider ourselves the primary ones called by God to impart His truth to the world. These are a few of the unspoken sentiments that are often characteristic of how pastors think of themselves within the disciple-making process.

So the notion that students are capable of offering valuable insights and perspectives pertaining to faith in Jesus Christ—and, in a way, of discipling their rabbi—feels counterintuitive to many establishment pastors. This is because the iron-epoch church and its pastors have often framed disciple making as an indoctrination of theological postulates imparted by theological authorities. While I affirm sound biblical theology, it is not enough for people of the clay-epoch to be indoctrinated with such truths; they must incarnate potential truths, testing a truth's validity through personal life experience. The typical clay-culture young adult argues that since the "truth" they have gained has been personally learned, experienced and validated, they are justified in believing that the disciple may indeed have practical theological insights worth contributing to his or her leaders. Be clear: this is not necessarily arrogance on their part. Nor is the young adult rebelling against those in authority. It is simply a different paradigm of how learning and the application of knowledge and truth occurs. This principle of collaboration and contribution extends into and beyond the mentorship relationship and beyond the classroom. It has now invaded the local church.

3

The Divide Deepens

CHANGE OR BE CHANGED—In the old ecology of nature, change was seen as abnormal. In the new ecology of nature, change is life's natural, normative state. . . . What works today won't work tomorrow. . . . The wonder is that churches are not in more disarray. . . . They are standing pat, opting to uphold the status quo rather than undergo the upheaval.

Leonard Sweet, *Soul Tsunami*

M any pastors, generally those from the boomer generation, do not fully comprehend the present cultural divide between the people of the iron-epoch and people of the clay-epoch. They do realize, however, that precious few young adults attend their services and programs. As a result, many pastors seek to connect with young adults by using today's new technology. Unfortunately, they often use that technology incorrectly and ultimately reinforce how out of touch they truly are with clay-epoch cultural values. This truth is abundantly evident by how pastors often use the Internet to showcase their ministry organization online.

Most church websites communicate little about Christ.

The advent of the Internet offers an unprecedented paradigm shift for extending Christ-centered ministry into the global world—all with an efficiency never before possible. Yet sadly, even though this global medium exists, most churches refuse to execute the Great Commission online and make this command of Christ their prime mission directive. Rather, they spend their time and resources promoting their own organization as opposed to truly relating Christ. A quick look at most church websites will betray a church's priorities. Most church websites communicate little about Christ. The majority of web content is almost exclusively focused upon the church institution, its staff and its programming. On December 20, 2000, the Pew Research Center's Internet and American Life Project reported in an article entitled "Congregations Say the Internet Helps their Spiritual and Community Life,"

> [Churches] are much more likely to use the Web for one-way communication features such as posting sermons or basic information, than they are to have two-way communications features or interactive features such as

spiritual discussions, online prayer, or fundraising. The most commonly used features on these Web sites are:

- 83% encourage visitors to attend.

- 77% post mission statements, sermons, or other text concerning their faith.

- 76% have links to denomination- and faith-related sites.

- 60% have links to Scripture studies or devotional material.

- 56% post schedules, meeting minutes and other internal communications.[1]

Little has changed since 2000. On most church websites the gospel of Jesus Christ is not even mentioned. And when it is, it represents a minor portion of the website. Almost never is there relational support offered in real time for those seeking to know Christ. Unlike the professional business world that commonly offers a live-help chat-room feature so that the website user can interact with a real person, many church websites don't even list an e-mail address or a phone number.

Furthermore, churches ought not to confuse a statement of faith with an evangelical presentation of the gospel. Prior to the boomer generation, evangelism was almost always a relational interaction between a believer and a non-believer. Whatever the motivation, the nonbeliever understood his or her need for Christ and knew that a Christian friend or pastor could help him or her enter into a faith relationship with Jesus Christ. Since the mid-1960s many evangelical churches have replaced relational evangelism with offering pamphlets, doctrinal statements or invitations to attend a "seeker service." The church has become anti-social when it comes to the work of "going into the world to make disciples," especially in regard to relating the gospel of Jesus Christ relationally via interactive websites.

I was not always so cynical. Prior to the events of 9/11, I was actually a proponent of the established church-growth principles espoused by television-influenced church-growth gurus. However, following the terrible proceedings of 9/11, the Lord led me to design one of the first web-based social-network systems available to the church called E-Church Essentials. My desire was to remove the obstacles preventing churches and pastoral leaders from literally "going" into all the world and making disciples. At that time George Barna had just released his study on the "cyberchurch."[2] Based upon his study, Barna determined that one of the primary benefits of the Internet for the body of Christ was the potential for online teaching and training. So one of my goals was to make global/relational teaching and training possible even for computer novices.

What I soon discovered, however, broke my heart. While not true of all pastors, many pastors who utilized my company's online tools contacted our office by e-mail or phone demanding to know why people from Russia, Malaysia, Africa and other distant parts of the planet were signing up on their church's ministry account . When I explained that most of the world does not have quality churches, educated pastors, Christian bookstores or access to Bibles, and that people around the world were starving to be mentored and discipled in Christ, many pastors would respond: "These are not my people! Get them off my account." How sad.

While in-the-box ministry strategies make use of only 3 percent of the potential ministry time allotted to us each week, the vast majority of our church-budget allocations support the staff, debt and resources necessary to produce this in-the-box programming.

The potential for global-kingdom impact was at these pastors' fingertips, yet all they cared about were those who could attend and financially support their local institution. When designing websites for churches, I consistently challenge pastoral leaders to make their website a platform for ministry. Unfortunately, almost without exception over the last sixteen years, church leaders cannot fathom how ministry could be accomplished via the Internet. They view their website as an online brochure to advertise their church. The cultural paradigm of these television-influenced pastors inhibit them from moving outside the box that their accepted paradigm perceives.

For pastoral leaders I often distinguish between in-the-box thinking and out-of-the-box thinking. "In the box" refers to what goes on inside the big boxes we call our worship centers. In-the-box thinking is concerned with drawing people into our service programs on specific days, at specific times and in specific big-box locations. In most churches, in-the-box activity accounts for approximately four to six hours of programmed "ministry" per week. Consequently, during the remaining 162 hours each week, our "boxes"—our church buildings—remain empty and unused. However, while in-the-box ministry strategies make use of only 3 percent of the potential ministry time allotted to us each week, the vast majority of our church-budget allocations support the staff, debt and resources necessary to produce this in-the-box programming. I have found that when I speak with pastors of the iron-realm culture and playfully assert that I could offer them a strategy to get ten thousand people to attend their church on Sunday mornings, most pastors would want to do whatever it takes to reach this many people within their "boxes. However, when I assert that they can actually reach over one hundred thousand people for Christ using out-of-the-box Internet-based strategies, most pastors are not interested.

Another reason that the "box" is an established and proven ministry paradigm is that the Internet is not only new, but it is becoming more "new" every day

---

So why do pastoral leaders believe in "boxes" so much and in the Internet so little?

Part of the reason is that the "box" is an established and proven ministry paradigm. Iron-realm pastors were typically raised in big-box churches and so they replicate what they know best. Another reason is that the Internet is not only relatively new (compared to television and radio) but it has the unique characteristic of becoming more new every day. As a result, the iron-epoch pastor cannot keep up with Internet developments.

When the Internet was first introduced to the boomers, the generation that most of these pastors come from, they experienced what has become known as Web 1.0. Web 1.0 was essentially the text-based e-mail and static websites from the early days of the Internet that offered a simple brochure-like monologue communication medium. As a result, websites gained a reputation of being merely electronic brochures—a form of marketing collateral. For many iron-epoch (mostly boomer) pastors, Web 1.0 defined for them the scope and limitations of the Internet. Therefore, the current design of many church websites reveals their Web 1.0 "online brochure" paradigm. Brochure websites are graphics-driven rather than content or relationship-driven.

One clear example out of thousands is from one of the largest and most influential churches in America. At the time this book was written, this church's home page was almost exclusively graphical, depicting a stage full of performers as the audience passively watched. It was clearly an online brochure. This kind of design severely inhibits search engines from properly categorizing the website. And because of this church's influence among many thousands of ministries, many churches have followed its misguided lead.

However, the Internet continues to evolve: "Tim Berners-Lee invented the World Wide Web in 1989. He created it as an interface for the Internet and a way for people to share information with one another."[3] From the static pages at the Internet's birth to its present user-interactive version, Web 2.0+, which is quickly morphing into Web 3.0, the Internet aggressively changes. Within a span of three to five years, many facets of the Internet will be different than they are currently. People of the clay-epoch culture are comfortable with change and expect it. In contrast, most people who represent the iron-epoch culture appear to be resistant to change.

What are Web 1.0, 2.0 and 3.0? As we touched on earlier, these are developmental generations of the Internet with profound systemic improvements. For example, HTML5 is a newly emerging Internet programming language that will make data acquisition and website interaction a smooth, seamless experience. The goal of HTML5, as I understand it, is eventually to be able to eliminate the need for website plugins such as Adobe Flash and the many other such Internet apps that are currently available. The website w3schools.com, a site dedicated to promoting and communicating emerging Internet trends, explains that HTML5 is designed to deliver almost everything you want to do online without requiring additional plugins. It does everything from animation to apps, music to movies, and can also be used to build complicated applications that run in the browser.[4]

Tim O'Reilly, who is often credited with helping create the term "Web 2.0," explains,

The concept of "Web 2.0" began with a conference brain-storming session between O'Reilly and MediaLive International. Dale Dougherty, web pioneer and O'Reilly VP, noted that far from having "crashed" [Supposed Dot-Com Bubble Crash of 2001], the web was more important than ever, with exciting new applications and sites popping up with surprising regularity. What's more, the companies that had survived the collapse seemed to have some things in common. Could it be that the dot-com collapse marked some kind of turning point for the web, such that a call to action such as "Web 2.0" might make sense? We agreed that it did, and so the Web 2.0 Conference was born.[5]

Because the Internet continues to transform, it is difficult to specifically define its evolving attributes. The following features clearly distinguish the current generations (Web 2.0 and above) from their text-based non-interactive predecessor, Web 1.0:

- *Social Networking.* Web 2.0+ is about nurturing and supporting online relationships. Social networking makes use of not only e-mail but also instant messaging, text messaging, video conferencing, Voice-over-Internet-Protocol (VoIP), blogs, chat rooms and discussion forums. The lines between cell phone and computer are quickly disappearing. We can make a phone call using our computer, or we can surf the Internet using our cell phone. Twitter.com, Facebook.com, and LinkedIn.com are but a few examples of popular social networking sites. In a slightly different genre, Skype.com provides free video conferencing and collaboration with other Skype.com members.

- *Interactive Virtual Environments.* These environments include online gaming, virtual shopping malls, virtual conferences that often contain virtual exhibitor booths, virtual dating, virtual coffeehouses and much more. All these virtual environments utilize an avatar, which is a graphical depiction or representation of the system user. In recent years Leonard Sweet has been experimenting with a virtual library/learning center for the Christian leadership market in which avatars may interact together in real time over various books and topics.

- *Mobile Media.* Downloading or streaming video, audio and pictures on portable media players and cell phones and sharing this media with an online social network has become extremely popular. Android and iPhone apps (formerly known as software applications) are abundant on the Internet, ready to be downloaded and installed on our cell phones to make media interaction even more fluid. Young adults no longer need to listen to radio stations via antenna-restricted devices that lose radio signals due to a limited range, because they can (and do) listen to most any radio station throughout the world via the Internet. As early as 2007, one in four Internet users (25 percent) regularly streamed radio from their laptop or desktop.[6] This number has vastly increased since then. With the advent of online tools such as Pandora, users can customize the kind of music they like to listen to. Aligning with this trend and in an effort to better utilize bandwidth, as of 2012 all American television is now 100 percent digital, making the integration of television into the Internet a coming reality.

- *Online Learning.* Relational e-learning and interactive webinars have become a mainstream instructional medium for corporations and educational institutions. Contrary to popular thought, however, online learning is not merely for large organizations. In fact, recent polls conducted by the eLearning Guild, the world's premier e-learning resource organization (www.elearningguild.com), have demonstrated that organizational size is not a determination of e-learning success within the current web generation. Yet if e-learning is to be effective it must have a strong relational component—mentor-to-student and peer-to-peer online community interaction is crucial.

- *Information Environments.* Search engines and wikis are very popular. A wiki is a website in which participating members may contribute information to the site based upon each member's area of expertise. Wikipedia.com is the classic example of an interactive wiki. Whether a search engine or a wiki, these informational environments create a general sense of global membership and a responsibility to contribute to and receive from the global information community.

- *Mobile Integration.* Everything is going mobile. All the functions listed above and more can now run from a smartphone. Mobile integration of software apps as well as integration into one's real-time daily life is and will be the norm for many decades to come.

When we examine these "together" and "one another" phrases closely and forget for the moment that we are talking about the Internet, it would not be difficult to imagine these same community values being practiced and espoused by the first-century Christian church.

The common thread among Web 2.0+ systems is an emphasis upon a relational community. In them we meet together, we share information together, we learn together, we share experiences together, and we support one another—with ever-evolving speed and ease. When we examine these "together" and "one another" phrases closely and forget for the moment that we are talking about the Internet, it would not be difficult to imagine these same community values being practiced and espoused by the first-century Christian church.

The clay-epoch culture does not advocate that online "togetherness" is a substitute for face-to-face relationships. This culture values authentic relationships as much as, if not more than, the iron-epoch culture. The difference is that the clay-epoch generation utilizes online tools to help discover, enhance and maintain their authentic relationships. Relationships are now forged around communities of shared interests rather than communities of shared geography. This is an important concept for church leaders to grasp, so I will repeat it: *communities form online and offline based upon shared interests rather than shared geography.* And these shared interests are now global in scope. The "community" church can no longer consider their local village as the limits of their ministry mission field. Similarly, churches that refuse to restructure themselves around co-communities of shared interests will find it difficult to attract and keep young adults.

In the language of Internet culture, a "troll" is an individual who posts off-topic, irrelevant and at times emotionally inflammatory messages within a shared-interest online community. I would submit that many pastors and churches are in danger of being labeled "troll churches" because they ignore the shared interests and communal values of people within the clay-epoch society and insist on presenting their message their way without consideration of the needs of the Internet-influenced culture they are trying to reach. However, when we meet people at their point of need, whether it is offline or online, the Holy Spirit can do an incredible work.

One powerful example of the Internet's relational-ministry potential was once offered by www.essentials.tv, a website sponsored by the North American Mission Board that is unfortunately now offline and disbanded. This site offered various videos for the promotion of evangelism and global missions. One of these videos told the story of how Becky and Lee came to abandon their Mormon faith and accept Jesus Christ as their Lord and Savior. The video is inspirational in its retelling of the many chat-room interactions between Becky, who felt that she would never be good enough to enter the celestial kingdom (Mormon heaven), and her relational pastor-mentor. Through six months of online Bible study, the pastor was able to introduce Becky to Jesus Christ. In turn Becky helped lead her husband to Christ. And since no Christian church existed in their Mormon community, they flew the pastor from Canada to Utah to help plant a new church in their area.

The ministry investment in Becky's life would not have been possible if it were not for the Internet. Her cloistered Mormon community was devoid of a Christian church. As a result, there was no place for her to go with her spiritual struggles except to an Internet community. For Becky, the Internet was culturally relevant, available at the times when she was most able to explore her spirituality (late at night) and, because of the faithfulness of just one pastor, highly relational.

One church that "gets it" is Life Church in Edmond, Oklahoma (LifeChurch.tv). Not only does this church minister online to people in ways that support shared-interest community ministry, it has also created various hosted software solutions to facilitate its online mission to others as well as facilitate the discipleship of those the ministry is reaching. These tools currently include:

- *YouVersion*—an interactive, community-based, mobile and online Bible (www.bible.com)

- *BibleX*—an interactive, community-based, Bible-study tool that facilitates spiritual exploration and maturation

- *Podcasts*—downloadable sermons and teachings as well as online groups to enable people to discuss the teachings in community

But LifeChurch.tv does not stop with creating online tools for individuals to use; it also creates free online software solutions for other churches to use—the church sees itself as an equipper of the church at large to facilitate global online ministry. LifeChurch.tv has become a benchmark example for other churches to follow.

In my experience most pastoral leaders are not familiar with these kinds of tools, or, if they know what they are, they refuse to utilize them. Why? For two reasons: (1) they do not understand the Internet culture, or (2) they are often simply too busy preparing for "presentational church" every Sunday to invest their time in interacting with people regarding spiritual matters. The North American institutional church and its pastors and staff often continue to perpetuate a ministry philosophy either dictated by the television-influenced generation or replicated upon these values because pastoral leaders do not know any better way for the local church to function. As a result, the spiritual inheritance given from people of the iron epoch to the people of the clay epoch is received as dysfunctional and countercultural in light of the divergent values held by people shaped by our Internet-influenced society.

4

A Dysfunctional Inheritance

Other people are going to find healing in your wounds.
Your greatest life messages and your most effective ministry
will come out of your deepest hurts.

Rick Warren

Clay-epoch believers tend to be mission-driven. They want to be personally involved in making a positive impact within their world. Yet let's be honest—young adults of every past generation, as they have been traditionally defined and labeled, have displayed a passion to make a difference in their world. The builder generation, also called the greatest generation, defeated fascism and communism. The boomer generation rebelled against the status quo and challenged social and racial injustices that devastated the self-worth of many minority groups. Generation X built upon the foundation laid by the overcoming of global and domestic injustice by opening the doors to innovation and driving better economies. Now it's time for the people of the clay epoch to make a significant difference in their world.

Unlike people in the iron epoch, young adults of the clay epoch have the tools and resources to make an incredible global impact. Yet in spite of such great potential, the typical church in America appears to inhibit this demographics' involvement at every turn. Rather than allow people of the clay-epoch culture to influence how ministry occurs within their big box, people of the iron-epoch culture insist on "blessing" the emerging generations with an inheritance that is generally not desired nor valued—that is, the boomer generation's television-influenced ministry model.

A growing number of people believe that there is something inherently unhealthy in the way we describe and practice church today. For example, God has called us to help build His kingdom, not build our own kingdoms through institutionalism. Now I'm certainly not an anarchist seeking to destroy organizational and systemic structures. But God designed me to serve as a systemologist. I believe in organizational structures. I firmly believe that we can accomplish much more for Christ when we serve together than we ever could by serving independently. My concern with our present institutional structures is that our mission and purpose seem to have strayed from God's mission and purpose. God instructs us to "go into the world," but the American church invites people to "come into our churches." God instructs church leadership to "equip people for ministry service." Church leadership prefers to recruit volunteers with little or no equipping to fill their programming holes. There seems to be a strong tendency within the iron-epoch church not only to do what seems right in their own eyes (see Judg. 21:25) but to also program and institutionalize the various movements of God's Spirit manifested within society.

The apostle Peter was once guilty of wanting to "institutionalize" the work of God. In Luke 9:32–34 we find the account of Jesus' meeting on the mountain:

> Peter and his companions were very sleepy, but when they became fully awake, they saw his glory and the two men standing with him. As the men were leaving Jesus, Peter said to him, "Master, it is good for us to be here. Let us put up three shelters—one for you, one for Moses and one for Elijah." (He did not know what he was saying.) While he was speaking, a cloud appeared and covered them, and they were afraid as they entered the cloud.

Clearly Peter had *Sukkot* (the Festival of Booths) in mind, possibly even the *ushpizin* prayers often recited during *Sukkot* inviting venerated Jewish leaders of the past to inhabit the booths during the festival. The text points out that Peter "did not know what he was saying." Similarly, today's institutional churches may not perceive correctly what they should be doing. Why are we so quick to build buildings to institutionalize God's work among His people? Why do we think God needs a "big box" to enshrine His work?

The "cloud" of God's Spirit within the elect is a far greater tabernacle than any facility that human hands might build. While there is nothing inherently wrong with a local body of Christ followers meeting within buildings, we may be in danger of missing the mark through misplaced priorities. This was not always the case with the boomer generation. God initiated some incredible movements of His Spirit during their time, but in each case many in the boomer generation sought to institutionalize and manage the Holy Spirit's work.

God has utilized the boomer generation, those born beginning in 1946, to make a significant impact upon this world for the sake of Christ. Unfortunately, this television-influenced generation has often strayed from God's original work through them. The task before the church now is to strip away the dysfunction that has evolved over the past decades while valuing and respecting the healthy inheritance left to us by previous generations.

Healthy Aspects of Our Inheritance

Now in their late sixties, the boomer generation embodies the last remnants of the iron-realm culture in America. As the spiritual leaders of this generation prepare for retirement, it is only appropriate to thank them for their faithful service and to remember what positive influences they have had upon us and the church. Our positive inheritance from them includes, but is not limited to, the Jesus Movement, the Charismatic Renewal, lay-ministry mobilization, the worship reformation and the small-group church-deconstruction movement. I believe that as we review the historic work of the Holy Spirit through this generation, we will discover elements within these various movements that are valued and utilized today within the clay-epoch culture.

Our Heritage: The Jesus Movement

The Jesus Movement of the late 1960s and '70s was inherently antiestablishment and anti-institutionalism. It was not so much about rebellion, as typified its generation. It was rather a counterculture reaction to the moral excesses of the '60s and '70s, one that inspired people to seek something more "real" and "authentic." The result was a growing desire by many to have a real and vital relationship with God through Jesus Christ and to exist in authentic Christ-centered community (Christian communes, coffeehouses, etc.).

The Jesus Movement was a spiritual revival. It was a grassroots spiritual movement not orchestrated by any organization but rather by the Holy Spirit. Significant parallels exist between the values and goals of the clay-epoch culture and the values and goals of the Jesus Movement decades ago. This parallel, I believe, is not merely '70s-retro spirituality but a call by God's Spirit to return to the place at which the church was once healthier. To help us objectively reflect upon the Jesus Movement era, let's look at some excerpts from a 1971 edition of *Time* magazine on which a depiction of Jesus made the cover because of this movement's impact upon American culture:

Some converts seem to enjoy translating their new faith into everyday life. . . . But their love seems more sincere than a slogan, deeper than the fast-fading sentiments of the flower children; what startles the outsider is the extraordinary sense of joy that they are able to communicate. . . . There are signs that the movement is something quite a bit larger than a theological Hula-Hoop, something more lasting than a religious Woodstock. It cuts across nearly all the social dividing lines, from crew cut to long hair, right to left, rich to poor. It shows considerable staying power: many who were in its faint beginnings in 1967 are still leading it. It has been powerful enough to divert many young people from serious drug addiction. Its appeal is ecumenical, attracting Roman Catholics and Jews, Protestants of every persuasion and many with no religion at all. Catholics visit Protestant churches with a new empathy, and Protestants find themselves chatting with nuns and openly enjoying Mass. "We are all brothers in the body of Christ," says a California Catholic lay leader, and he adds: "*We are on the threshold of the greatest spiritual revival the U.S. has ever experienced.*"[1]

The Jesus Movement and our present clay epoch share three common values:

1. An emphasis upon spiritual and relational authenticity

2. An emphasis upon social impact and justice

3. An anti-institutional grassroots influence for church transformation

I find it interesting that some boomers, whose generation was shaped in part by the values of the Jesus Movement, now tend to criticize clay-epoch Christ followers for seeking to lay claim to the same spiritual values and goals the Jesus Movement once espoused.

Our Heritage: The Charismatic Renewal

The Charismatic Renewal was a direct outgrowth of the Jesus Movement. During this time the church rediscovered the real and vital activity of the Holy Spirit within the life of the common individual Christ follower. The Holy Spirit did not value dead institutionalism. The Holy Spirit could not be contained in a human plan or a routine program as typified by so many church services both then and now. It was an amazing honor that the Holy Spirit would be willing to move in and through His people in order to accomplish His good work. The church learned in this movement that the supernatural should be expected; it should be normative. After all, it is in the Holy Spirit's nature to be supernatural. The Charismatic Renewal also crossed denominational boundaries. People were charismatic, not churches. Yes, there were Pentecostal churches, but the Charismatic Renewal applied primarily to a spiritual revival among people within non-Pentecostal mainline Protestant and Catholic churches.[2] This influence led to a renewed sensitivity to the Holy Spirit's work within the life of local mainline congregations.

Time magazine recorded the impact of this movement in 1977 when it reported on the nation's first charismatic ecumenical conference:

In the troubled '60s there began to appear the "neo-Pentecostalists," most of whom prefer to be known as Charismatics. They share Parham's belief in baptism by the Holy Spirit, but they prefer to remain in their own churches rather than join a Pentecostal church. They are predominantly white and middle class, and they are growing rapidly. . . . Some good old-fashioned body-swaying, arm-waving, eye-rolling times were had last week in Kansas City as 45,000 members of the Charismatic Christian movement met in their first interdenominational assembly. Said Kevin Ranaghan, a Roman Catholic who was chairman of the conference: *I believe this is the largest grass-roots ecumenical movement in 800 years.*[3]

Once again, the movement of God's Spirit is described here as initiated and supported by the "grassroots." This is also a key value shared by the clay-epoch culture, a culture filled with people shaped by the Internet that has empowered individuals (as opposed to institutions) at a grassroots level. The clay-epoch culture resonates with the belief that God could work directly through individuals and groups of individuals apart from formal institutions.

Today individuals have the potential for significant global contribution through the Internet. The same fervency of Spirit-directed personal ministry, once celebrated during the charismatic movement, is taking new form among the people of the clay-epoch culture. This culture needs to experience a real God working in real lives; anything short of this kind of experiential faith is likely to receive little respect from today's young people.

Yet today many of our churches put God into a one-hour, highly programmed "box" planned in fifteen-second increments and supported with additional institutionalized programming. In many of our iron-epoch churches, personal ministry is anything but grassroots. Personal ministry in many churches is only blessed by the church leadership if it fills the staffing holes within the current programming. I consistently hear boomer-generation pastors ridicule today's young adults as not dependable and uncommitted. What they are rightly saying is that they cannot depend upon today's young adults to commit to and support their institutional top-down controlled programs.

Today's typical "corporate" church is anti-grassroots. In this regard it is also anti-personal ministry and anti-Internet influenced. The clay-epoch counterculture naturally distances itself from these perceived dysfunctions. Today's iron-epoch American church would be a foreign and objectionable thing if viewed through the eyes of the 1970s charismatic Christian, who sought to reform the stale highly structured mainline institutions of their day.

Unlike the Charismatic Renewal movement of the 1970s, however, people of the clay-epoch culture are far less passionate about reforming church institutions from within. Rather than work within current systems, they opt to build their own spiritual constructs theologically and ecclesiastically. Theological experimentalism by today's young adults has been harshly criticized by iron-epoch church leaders, and in some cases for good reason. However, ecclesiastical experimentalism is the natural consequence of an overwhelming insensitivity by iron-epoch boomer-generation leaders to the vision and values of Christ followers within the clay-epoch culture. Why the exodus? Denominational studies show that only about 5 percent of the people who serve and make decisions within our current institutions are post-boomers.[4] In essence, the voice of the clay-epoch culture has been all but silenced within many churches.

"After all," iron epoch-leaders muse, "why change? Look at our megachurch! Has God not blessed our way of doing ministry?"

Sadly, this "father knows best" attitude is unleashing the laity right out the back door of our established churches.

Julia Duin, in her book *Quitting Church*, analyzed why people, particularly people under age thirty, are exiting the local church. In a beliefnet.com interview, she made the following remarks about the need for relevant church methodologies that help young adults experience the reality of the Holy Spirit at work in their lives:

> Part of the problem is that pastors do not want to admit that much of Christianity does not work. So many of the promises in Scripture simply don't come true, and people cannot wrap their minds around that contradiction. Now, there are ways around this, but it's the rare pastor who gets it that people are struggling with what their lives are like and what the Bible says— and the wide gulf in between. . . . After a while people think they must be awful Christians because the system is not working for them, so they drop out of sheer

discouragement. That does not need to happen, yet this goes on all the time. Folks hate being part of something in which all they do is fail.

I was part of the Jesus movement and the charismatic renewal, so I have seen how wonderful Christianity was back in the halcyon days of revival in the 1970s. I know things can be better. I have experienced Jesus myself; I have learned to hear His voice, and it is nonsense to say He has failed."[5]

Our Heritage: Lay-Ministry Mobilization

The charismatic movement made the church aware of biblical teachings regarding the use of spiritual giftedness among the people. However, this emphasis intensified as biblical scholars working on the New International Version of the Bible in the early and mid-1970s discovered, with the aid of the newly recovered Dead Sea Scrolls, that Ephesians 4:12 had often been mistranslated. They now realized that it was the responsibility of pastors, teachers and evangelists *to equip the laity* so that the laity—rather than the pastors—might be empowered to do the works of ministry service. Contrast the 1970s biblical scholarship view with the classical King James translation of verses 11–13:

> He gave some, apostles; and some, prophets; and some, evangelists; and some, pastors and teachers; [the leaders exist] for the perfecting of the saints, [the leaders exist] for the work of the ministry, [the leaders exist] for the edifying of the body of Christ: till we all [the people and the leaders] come in the unity of the faith, and of the

knowledge of the Son of God, unto a perfect man, unto the measure of the stature of the fulness of Christ. (KJV)

Christ himself gave the apostles, the prophets, the evangelists, the pastors and teachers, to equip his people for works of service, so that the body of Christ may be built up until we all reach unity in the faith and in the knowledge of the Son of God and become mature, attaining to the whole measure of the fullness of Christ. (NIV)

Everyone's spiritual job description was now rewritten. People realized that the responsibility of church leadership was to *equip*. The responsibility of the people was to *do the ministry* according to their God-ordained giftedness. Suddenly spiritual-gift surveys proliferated within the church. Discovering one's gift or gifts was considered essential to spiritual maturity.

This movement was not birthed in an effort to fill holes within elaborate church programs. This was a movement in which ministry service often occurred apart from institutionally driven programs and church structures. Only after it was underway did church leaders deviate from the God-ordained role of equipping and begin to administrate programs that artificially utilized people's giftedness to fill programming holes. Rather than permit the human-resource pool of God-ordained giftedness to define a church's ministry, today we often have programs that require particularly gifted people and exclude people who are not gifted according to the needs of the program. All too often if an individual's ministry calling does not fit within the institution's prescribed programming structures, the individual's ministry potential is simply ignored by church staff.

Furthermore, our churches often institute artificial and subjective standards of professionalism. People who cannot meet these subjective standards on their own are not generally equipped by ministry staff to do so. More often than not they are simply rejected from participating within the ministry programming at all. Even if it can be argued that professionalism is a legitimate value, the church must come to terms with the reality that today very little "equipping" ever occurs to help the lay person become more professional—let alone more effective and obedient to the call of Christ within his or her life.

In fact, in a 2008 survey I conducted of 650 pastoral leaders, only three churches were able to articulate any kind of intentional equipping-for-ministry strategy. Clearly, in most iron-epoch churches, equipping people to discover and fulfill God's ministry calling upon their life is not a high priority. When I speak with pastors regarding this deficiency, they typically respond either defensively, arguing that their Sunday sermons are "equipping," or they humbly acknowledge that they were never personally equipped for ministry within a local church and so do not know what this kind of program should look like.

This is a sad statement on several levels but most specifically to our discussion, because young adults would value being mentored and coached to become effective for Christ—as long as the end result of the coaching is that they can actually experience for themselves what being effective looks and feels like.

Our Heritage: The Worship Reformation

It was the boomer generation who first taught the church that worship was not about forms or liturgy. Worship could be real, heartfelt and authentic. Gone was the pipe organ. Enter the culturally-relevant Hammond B3 organ, the Fender Rhodes piano and the guitars and drums of the 1970s and '80s. Worship songs by the thousands were written and distributed without a commercial music-distribution network in place. The songs were simple, often just Scripture put to music, but they helped turn the hearts of people to their God.

Worship services often went on for hours. Worship was not about performance. Even band members were typically more concerned with worshiping God than with performing perfectly. It is likely that the simplicity of the music in that era freed musicians to focus less on themselves and their instruments and more upon their Lord. This kind of new worship in its earliest iteration was like a flowing and unstoppable river—a great movement of God's Spirit within His church, calling the hearts of each worshiper to His heart. The fervor of worship at that time gave birth to theological constructs such as *Worship Evangelism* by Sally Morgenthaler.

But something changed. "Fervor" doesn't exactly describe what woefully passes today for worship within many churches. In many churches worship bands seem more

interested in performing—gigging—than in worshiping.
Our services have become so programmed and regimented
that it is now possible to go from church to church (and
many people do) and know exactly what is going to take
place, what songs will be sung, without ever looking at a
service program. Week after week, service after service, the
process is spiritually stifling in its redundancy and routine.
Sally Morgenthaler, disillusioned by how churches had
institutionalized her philosophy of worship evangelism and
desiring for people who did not know Christ to be attracted
to Him because they observed Christ followers authentically
loving and worshiping their Lord, disbanded her website
Sacramentis. She described her visits to churches that had
institutionalized her formula in a *Rev!* magazine interview:

> By 2002 a few pastors of praise and worship churches
> began admitting to me that they weren't making much
> of a dent in the surrounding non-Christian population,
> even though their services were packed and they were
> known for the best worship production in town. Several
> asked me to help them crack the unchurched code. One
> wanted to invest in an expensive VJ machine and target
> twentysomethings. The others thought multisensory,
> ancient-future, or emergent twist might help. However,
> when I visited their congregations, it wasn't hard to see
> that the biggest barrier to reaching the unchurched had
> little to do with worship technique or style. It had to do
> with isolation and the faux-worship that isolation inevi-
> tably creates. . . . Too many times, I came away with an
> unnamed, uneasy feeling. Something was not quite right.

The worship felt disconnected from real life. Then there were the services when the pathology my friend talked about came right over the platform and hit me in the face. It was unabashed self-absorption, a worship culture that screamed "It's all about us" so loudly that I wondered how any visitor could stand to endure the rest of the hour.[6]

Our Heritage: The Small-Group Church-Deconstruction Movement

In the early 1980s the churches led by iron-realm boomers began to refine the methodologies birthed in the movements previously listed. Some may rightfully claim that all these diverse movements were only perspectives of one great movement of God's Spirit. Yet the very thing that the Jesus-movement boomers previously reviled—institutionalism—was now the driving force within the American church.

Some of the responsibility for this shift in values should rightfully go to iron-epoch, boomer-led churches who so aptly taught American churches how to institutionalize their "operations" as corporations did and to program their services to be like television productions. It's not that these churches should be condemned. God has used them in many positive ways. But as the historic Israelites traded leadership by God for a human leader with human structures, so too have iron-epoch churches traded surrender to God's Spirit for human institutional church-growth models. And for a while, the church-growth models seemed to justify the trade by their apparent effectiveness. Churches were growing in greater numbers than ever before, and the megachurch movement was born. However, the trade came at a great price. High growth rates did not present corresponding relational or spiritual growth. People felt isolated and alone within a crowd of thousands.

In seeking a solution to the relational dilemma, American megachurches turned to a small-group model that originated in Korea (where some of the largest megachurches existed) by an Assemblies of God pastor and chairman of the World Assemblies of God Fellowship, Dr. David Yonggi Cho. People may know this movement as that of small groups, cell groups, metachurch, microchurch or home church, but in the end these labels all describe one thing: the deconstruction of the organized institutional church into smaller relational entities. Church-growth gurus began to use expressions such as "Get small to get big!" However, this expression missed the point. Small groups were not a way to create growth in congregation size. Small groups more closely resembled what the typical New Testament church was originally like.

How can we continue to follow church leaders who no longer separate the work of the Holy Spirit from the institutional life of their organization?

It was not uncommon in the early days of this movement to hear pastors promote small-group ministry by telling their congregations that "real ministry happens in small groups." When I hear such statements, I often wonder, *If this is true, then why do we need the big group with its big productions and even bigger financial overhead?*

Today there are many healthy small groups but far fewer healthy small-group ministry programs. It is common to find small-group programs that do not equip the small-group leaders at all or that provide only minimal equipping at best. Many church small groups exist as isolated spiritual islands in a vast sea of institutional programming.

It's Time to Strip Away the Dysfunction

The five ministry movements previously discussed began with simplicity and authenticity but became corrupted over time by people's desire to program and institutionalize the good things that God had set in motion. Now it is time to strip away the dysfunction and, following the lead of the prophet Nehemiah, reconstruct the true spiritual walls of Christ's church that have broken down. How can we continue to follow church leaders who no longer separate the work of the Holy Spirit from the institutional life of their organization? A case in point is Wayne Jacobsen's response to Tim Stafford's assertions in a 2005 *Christianity Today* article titled "The Church—Why Bother?" Here is a portion of Jacobsen's letter:

> What many of us have found on the outside offers more connection, more transformation, more opportunities for ministry than we ever found inside. Does it ever bother you that if Jesus wanted us to be part of these institutions with morning services, he did nothing in the Gospels to prepare

his disciples for it? On the contrary his example and words were far more de-centralized than that. Love each other as you've been loved. Where two or three of you get together I'll be there with you. He didn't envision church as a building, an institution or a service. He viewed it as a company of people following him, sharing his life with each other and serving the world with compassion and humility. For the first 300 years in the life of the church believers met in homes and would never have conceived of the Lord's Supper being served anywhere other than the family table.[7]

What was begun by the Holy Spirit during the coming of age of the boomer generation was awesome in its vitality, scope and impact. But that generation, for the most part, has now become part of an iron-epoch culture that desires to package God's work into something marketable, manageable and reproducible—and then enshrine the package within a giant building campaign. This has resulted in corruptions that will likely impact the North American church negatively for decades to come.

In the iron-epoch, boomer-led church model, the pastoral staff is comprised of the experts who tell, instruct and direct the unlearned. However, the Internet-influenced culture prefers "ex-*perts*" over experts. Someone who is *pert* is defined by the Merriam-Webster Dictionary as "saucily free and forward, flippantly cocky and assured, being trim and chic." The clay-epoch culture cares little about "pastoral-perts" who are cocky, self-assured and image-conscious chic. The clay-epoch culture seeks spiritual leaders who are willing to put aside their image facades and become real,

vulnerable and authentic Christ followers who see themselves as merely coworkers for Christ.

Brian Zahnd, founder and senior pastor of Word of Life
Church in St. Joseph, Missouri, often tells the story of his
transition from leader expert to spiritual facilitator when
he speaks at leadership conferences. He recounts how he
had a spiritual meltdown prior to preaching one Sunday
morning. Brian conveys how he was internally conflicted
between his desire to represent the biblical ideal and a deep
realization of his own spiritual inadequacies. As a result,
Brian determined before God no longer to convey perfected sermons but simply to convey how God was working
within his own life. To Brian's amazement, the more honest
and real he became about how God was working within his
life, the more people identified with his spiritual struggles.
What was the result? The church grew as never before.[8]

Christ's Church Has Paid the Price—Now Who Will Pay the Mortgage?

The builder and boomer generations supported building campaigns that are necessary to institutional ministry.
Due to the inflated population numbers in these two generations, the values and pocketbooks of the builders and
boomers are what has reshaped the landscape of the American church. Together they provide the financial support
base for huge building projects and their associated mortgages. In stark contrast the subsequent generations were the
first to display a significant decrease in population growth,
as seen in the following illustration:[9]

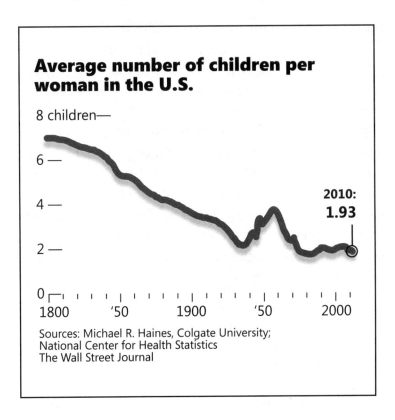

Average number of children per woman in the U.S.

8 children—

6 —

4 —

2 —

0

1800 · · · | · · · | · · · | · · · |
      '50   1900   '50   2000

2010:
1.93

Sources: Michael R. Haines, Colgate University;
National Center for Health Statistics
The Wall Street Journal

Clearly in the next couple of decades, most of the builder generation will die, and the boomer generation will move into a fixed-income retirement stage of life. These are not the generations that will build the future of the church. Retirement will take its financial toll on our inflated budgets, budgets that are inflated due to expensive buildings, expensive programming and expensive staff. Within the next ten years, churches must come to depend upon the people of the clay-epoch culture, or they will die.

But consider this: most of our churches have very few young adults currently in attendance, let alone in key leadership roles. The young adults between the ages of seventeen and thirty-five make up approximately 35 percent of our population nationally, but most churches are lucky if they average 10 percent attendance by this group. This is not a foundation upon which to maintain, never mind build, the future of our ministries. Millennials are abandoning the institutional churches they were raised in. The Barna Group studies the various culture shifts experienced within generational and subgenerational periods. It offers this summary:

> Loyalty to congregations is one of the casualties of young adulthood: twentysomethings were nearly 70% more likely than older adults to strongly assert that if they "cannot find a local church that will help them become more like Christ, then they will find people and groups that will, and connect with them instead of a local church." They are also significantly less likely to believe that "a person's faith in God is meant to be developed by involvement in a local church."[10]

This generation tells us that they distrust organized institutions and institutional leadership. So while studies show that the millennials' interest in spirituality is at an all-time high,[11] the spiritual inheritance that the iron-epoch churches cherished so much and sought to pass down to the next generation has been rejected.

Institutional churches should expect their membership demographic to significantly age and decline over the next fifteen years. Disproportionately, church budgets will decline, resulting in fewer staff and programming services. Churches that do not pay off their mortgages within the next fifteen years will be at serious financial risk. Even those institutional megachurches that do find a way to financially survive will struggle with ever-shrinking attendance within their cavernous big-box walls. Like it or not, the institutional church in America will be forced to deconstruct into smaller grassroots entities that can better relate to people, equip believers and collaborate together for the sake of Christ's kingdom.

We see this trend already taking place with the rising popularity of "satellite" or "campus" churches. This model plants multiple regional ministries rather than building a one-location megachurch. Each satellite ministry typically cooperates with one another and supports one another with practical, financial and human resources. The corporate-model church with its top-down hierarchy will soon be challenged to adopt a down-up structure that emphasizes the contributive role of each individual within the grassroots, just as is normative within the Internet.

The present deconstruction trend is not only influenced by financial constraints and mission goals, it is also influenced by relational Internet structures. In the Internet culture a "big" organization is generally a social network consisting of many small entities. The reason that the Internet is so pervasive is that it is not institutionally or hierarchically controlled. The Internet empowers the grassroots of humanity to dream their impossible dreams.

Entrepreneurialism in its many forms has exploded since 1995 as a direct result of the Internet. Effective pastors in the clay-epoch culture might do well to adopt a mind-set and methodology similar to that of Bill Gates, founder of Microsoft. The Microsoft Corporation does not develop and sell any end products. Rather, they became successful by developing resource tools that empowered grassroots individuals to develop their own end-user solutions. For example, I used Microsoft Word to write this book. Word is the tool that I used to create my book, the end-user product. Without a tool similar to Microsoft Word, writing a book would be far more laborious than it is. In short, the mission of Microsoft is to resource and equip people to be effective in their individual life-mission. Their website, www.microsoft.com, conveys a mission statement whose format any healthy church could adopt:

> At Microsoft, our mission is to *enable people and businesses* throughout the world *to realize their full potential.* We consider our mission statement a commitment to our customers. We deliver on that commitment by striving to create technology that is accessible to everyone—of all ages and abilities.[12]

Microsoft adopted a secular version of the Ephesians 4 mandate given to pastors, teachers, evangelists and apostles. Let's rework the Microsoft mission statement in a manner that may be applicable to Christ's church:

> At our church, our mission is to *enable people and ministry*

organizations throughout the world *to realize their full kingdom potential.* We consider our mission statement a commitment to those we serve and to Christ our Lord. We deliver on that commitment by *striving to equip and resource people* for kingdom ministry service—people of all ages and abilities.

I firmly believe that Christ's church would have far greater impact in this world, particularly within the Internet-influenced culture, if its leaders would adopt the "Microsoft model" within their churches. Adopting the Microsoft model will require a significant paradigm shift for both church leaders and church attendees. Leaders and churches who adopt this paradigm shift will no longer merely invite people to come and passively attend programmed services. Rather, these ministries will be transformed into training centers, empowering people with the resources, tools and equipping they require to make an incredible impact for Christ within this world. The reciprocal is also true. Grassroots individuals will be empowered to develop resources and tools for ministry and to train others how to use these resources to create their own end-user ministry solutions.

This paradigm shift cannot merely be a slogan our leaders tack onto their present institutionalized structures. The local church will need to transform every aspect of what it does and how it does it to ensure that the slogan becomes reality within the life of every church member. The vast majority of our time and our human and financial resources will no longer be invested into weekend productions. Passive observers will no longer represent the majority of those who attend our churches. Instead, the church's resources would be invested into (1) people development, (2) resource distribution and (3) human-resource deployment. The culture of the local church would then become one that celebrates the individual's "end-user product"—what he or she accomplishes for Christ's kingdom—rather than celebrating how good the service was on a given day or how we liked the music.

A church patterned after our modified mission statement will also adopt the responsibility to create the "tools" to empower teams of individuals to serve Christ effectively and to train each individual how to use the tools effectively. One church that currently strongly depicts this mission is LifeChurch.tv. When a person first interacts with their 2014 website, he or she will notice that it does not promote the qualities of the church organization but focuses upon the needs of the individual.

The website presents three doorways for the user: "New Here?" "What We Support" and "Resources." The textual content associated with each doorway emphasizes a global mission and personal involvement in that mission. In addition, LifeChurch.tv has made a serious investment in developing Internet tools for churches, individuals and families to help facilitate their global mission. It also exists as a multi-campus ministry—including a relational Internet campus. This is a relatively new and refreshing understanding of how Christ's church is to function in the clay-epoch culture. Ministries such as LifeChurch.tv are benchmarks that current churches and church plants should seek to emulate—not as a new church-growth model but as a conceptual template for how a global ministry can connect with and equip its people to make a planet-wide impact for Christ.

To sum up, the boomer ministry values of the 1970s definitely resonate with the clay-epoch culture. In this respect a '70s-retro mentality can provide a measure of mutual respect and understanding between the various cultural generations. In essence, to borrow from a 1980s-era popular movie theme, in some respects we can go "back to the future."

5

Defining Biblical Ministry in the Internet-Influenced Culture

*As I look back over fifty years of ministry, I recall
innumerable tests, trials and times of crushing pain. But
through it all, the Lord has proven faithful, loving, and
totally true to all his promises.*

David Wilkerson

Typically, leaders who advocate various ministry models do so because they are passionate about helping Christ's church become more effective in advancing His kingdom in this world. Yet naysayers of each model can find "biblical" and "practical" reasons that the proposed model should not be utilized. The American church tends to get caught up in dissecting the conflicting styles and methods associated with ministry models and will quickly attack those who do not support its preferred methodology.

It has not been my intention to attack any generation or style of church. Rather, my heart's desire is to proclaim with as large a megaphone as possible that *institutional church models that have worked in the past will no longer work for our future.*

Our cultural context has shifted dramatically. Yet it's also still very important that we do not lose sight of the core values essential to any biblically based Christ-centered ministry. Let's begin our definition of ministry by considering four presuppositions that I hope will help us come to agreement on what qualifies as true biblical ministry within Christ's church, regardless of our cultural preferences.

Presupposition 1: *The New Testament defines the mission directives for Christ's church.*

These include:

1. *Evangelism.* "Therefore go" (Matt. 28:19). "You will receive power when the Holy Spirit comes on you; and you will be my witnesses in Jerusalem, and in all Judea and Samaria, and to the ends of the earth" (Acts 1:8).

2. *Disciple making through teaching.* "Make disciples of all nations . . . teaching them to obey everything I have commanded you" (Matt. 28:19–20). "For everything that was written in the past was written to teach us, so that through the endurance taught in the Scriptures and the encouragement they provide we might have hope" (Rom. 15:4). "Let the message of Christ dwell among you richly as you teach and admonish one another with all wisdom through psalms, hymns, and songs from the Spirit, singing to God with gratitude in your hearts" (Col. 3:16).

3. *Christ-centered community.* "[Baptize] them in the name of the Father and of the Son and of the Holy Spirit" (Matt. 28:20). "While they were eating, Jesus took bread, and when he had given thanks, he broke it and gave it to his disciples, saying, 'Take and eat; this is my body.' Then he took a cup, and when he had given thanks, he gave it to them, saying, 'Drink from it, all of you. This is my blood of the covenant, which is poured out for many for the forgiveness of sins. I tell you, I will not drink from this fruit of the vine from now on until that day when I drink it new with you in my Father's kingdom'" (Matt. 26:26–29).

4. *Equipping and mobilizing people into ministry service.* "Surely I am with you always, to the very end of the age" (Matt. 28:20). "Christ himself gave the apostles, the prophets, the evangelists, the pastors and teachers, to equip his people for works of service, so that the body of Christ may be built up until we all reach unity in the faith and in the knowledge of the Son of God and become mature, attaining to the whole measure of the fullness of Christ" (Eph. 4:11–13).

5. *Loving and forgiving one another.* "'Teacher, which is the greatest commandment in the Law?' Jesus replied: '"Love the Lord your God with all your heart and with all your soul and with all your mind." This is the first and greatest commandment. And the second is like it: "Love your neighbor as yourself." All the Law and the Prophets hang on these two commandments'" (Matt. 22:36–40). "Do not judge, and you will not be judged. Do not condemn, and you will not be condemned. Forgive, and

you will be forgiven" (Luke 6:37). "A new command I give you: Love one another. As I have loved you, so you must love one another. By this everyone will know that you are my disciples, if you love one another" (John 13:34–35).

Presupposition 2: *Ministry, guided by our New Testament mission directives, happens best in the context of authentic relationships.*

Any ministry strategy that does not rely heavily upon building authentic relationships will likely have little ministry impact. The Bible tells us to "do everything in love" (1 Cor. 16:14). In Galatians 5:6 we are told that "the only thing that counts is faith expressing itself through love." While it may be possible to express faith outside relationships, it is impossible to love outside relationships. Authentic relationships are central to any true ministry strategy and so relational authenticity, expressed in sincere love, must also be central to any ministry strategy that the local church may implement.

For over two thousand years, basic missiology principles have taught the church that when we infiltrate an established culture, we must learn to understand the culture and adapt how we communicate our vital message—both in word and deed—in a manner that can be received by the culture.

Presupposition 3: *Ministry succeeds best when we tailor our communications methodologies to the values of our immediate culture.*

Unfortunately, the American church has not, for the

most part, effectively integrated itself into current culture. In the past churches often sought to create Christian sub-cultures. We have Christian music, a subculture of all other kinds of music. We have Christian movies, a subculture of all other movies. We have Christian cruises, a subculture of all other cruises. I could go on and on.

An objection is likely raised in your mind: "We are to be in the world but not of the world!" This is true. We are not to be of the world. However, the New Testament consistently uses the phrase "the world" to refer to a faith-less lifestyle that rejects the truth of redemption by Jesus Christ and sanctification by His Spirit. Rather than pull away from the culture to create our own subcultures, the Great Commission (see Matt. 28:18–20) assumes that we will *invade* the culture—that we will go (the active form of "go" is "in your going") *into* the world. For over two thousand years, basic missiology principles have taught the church that when we infiltrate an established culture, we must learn to understand the culture and adapt how we communicate our vital message—both in word and deed—in a manner that can be received by the culture.

This principle also suggests, as this book argues, that when a church has a website or a Facebook page or streams its sermons online, the church should not deceive itself that it is being relevant. These mediums, if overlaid upon a television-culture church, will be perceived by people of the Internet epoch as mere "window dressing." Because of this fact, it is very difficult for me to conceive of a *blended* church model whereby iron-epoch and clay-epoch people worship together. The cultural preferences of these two people groups are contrary to one another. This cultural division is about more than personal preferences over worship-music style, it is the result of a global epoch's intrusion into society.

For example, several centuries ago the people of the written-word epoch, established by the invention of the printing press, developed a ministry culture entirely unique from that of those who could not read. And those who could read and write in Latin developed a ministry culture unique from those individuals who could only read in what was considered to be a vulgar language. We need to break down the walls of our subcultures and learn again how to communicate our vital message in word and deed in a manner that can be received by the culture.

Presupposition 4: *Ministry must always be biblically informed and doctrinally sound.*

I find it interesting that among the people of the Internet-influenced culture, there is a revival of Reformed theology. During the waning years of the television-influenced church, there was great concern expressed by pastors and theologians alike that people were "feeling" their way through faith in Christ, that people were more concerned with feel-good experiences than with solid doctrine. A "feel-good faith" is an inadequate one when a global community challenges people to consider things such as, for example, the profound differences between Islam and Christianity. The worldviews of these two religions hold doctrines that are contradictory to one another. As a result, in a global community in which there exists a free exchange of ideas, people must decide for themselves what they believe and why they believe as they do.

Even while people of the Internet-influenced culture tend to hold that truth is relative, those who are sincere spiritual explorers will need to discover for themselves spiritual truth in both doctrine *and* experience. Spiritual experience must be real, sound and dependable, rooted in something deeper than self-satisfaction. The desire for this inspires some Internet-influenced people to revert to a "vintage faith" associated with either the first-century church or the early Reformation period, eras in which Christians upheld belief systems that truly impacted how they lived and worshiped. The impassioned doctrinal positions espoused by Calvin and Luther, beliefs that the Reformers risked their lives to uphold, offers a vision of clarity and conviction that is appealing to people who struggle to exist in a hedonistic society that promotes a murky, relativistic diversity.

The appeal of vintage faith transcends denominational divisions and distinctions. People of the Internet-influenced church perceive themselves solely in terms of a global society. Church organizations that promote their own institution or their denominational affiliation above the church universal will find it difficult to attract and retain Internet-influenced people within their congregations. The renewed emphasis people now place upon the church universal has resulted in the promotion of foundational Christian doctrines that Christ followers have held in common for centuries.

Historic church creedal statements such as the Apostles'
Creed typify these foundational doctrinal beliefs and have
been revived within the Internet-influenced church.

The Gospel Coalition is one example of an online ministry that is Reformed in doctrine while also emphasizing
core biblical doctrine. The ministry's preamble communicates the following:

> Our desire is to serve the church we love by inviting all
> our brothers and sisters to join us in an effort to renew
> the contemporary church in the ancient gospel of Christ
> so that we truly speak and live for him in a way that
> clearly communicates to our age. As pastors, we intend
> to do this in our churches through the ordinary means
> of his grace: prayer, the ministry of the Word, baptism
> and the Lord's Supper and the fellowship of the saints.
> We yearn to work with all who, in addition to embracing
> the confession and vision set out here, seek the lordship
> of Christ over the whole of life with unabashed hope in
> the power of the Holy Spirit to transform individuals,
> communities, and cultures.[1]

I personally uphold and advocate the doctrinal positions advocated by the Gospel Coalition. However, I realize
that not all Internet-influenced young adults would agree
with my presupposition that ministry must be biblically informed. There are many within the clay-epoch culture who,
when it comes to spiritual things, begin with self and their
own self-perceptions regarding life values and then feel free
to reject Christ's church or biblical doctrine whenever it
s not agree with their established preconceptions. But

this is nothing new. Cultures for generations have elevated self, even at times to a deistic level.

However, the concern regarding this is magnified at this time within the iron-epoch establishment church because members of this generation see their children, who were raised within their television-influenced churches, adopting the values that pagan society holds. There has been a deep failure in many television-influenced churches to teach people to obey all that Jesus commanded us (see Matt. 28:19-20). Rather, these kinds of churches have entertained people in hope of retaining numbers while all the while losing the souls of their very children.

Let's look at one example of a young self-deist adult and how he, and many others like him, justify his theology in his blog post entitled "I Am My Own God, Death to the Cross":

> It's really bothersome that people remember Jesus by the way he died rather than the way he lived. . . . Let's take Jesus off the cross and pay attention to the words he spoke. Man translated Jesus' death in a way that makes them feel less guilty. They claim he died for our sins and this couldn't be further from the truth. Let's be honest with ourselves, if this is truth and we still believe in sin then Jesus' death was in vain. For the highly devout this is blasphemous, for the rational mind one must then ask the question, "If Jesus didn't die for humanity's sins, then why did he die the way he did?" The answer is simple. He challenged the very foundation of society. . . . In the single phrase "I am God" he took the church's authority and opened

the door for everyone to find God within themselves. . . . People are so willing to give up their own divinity to an institution that cares only for power and monetary gain. Jesus urged humanity to look within one's own heart for God. The kingdom of heaven he said is within. . . . When God is found within there is no need to look outward, no church is needed.[2]

The iron-epoch television-influenced church cannot reach this young adult, but a clay-epic Internet-influenced church possibly could. The world simply needs a greater concentration of Internet-influenced churches that will not abandon sound doctrine upon the altar of relevancy and will likewise share in that same courage of faith displayed so long ago by Reformation leaders who were willing to invade their culture for Christ, no matter the cost.

6

The Church Service?

Whatever the reason, many younger leaders are turning from seeker-sensitive forms toward recapturing ambiguity and antiquity. . . . The focus now is on authenticity of religious experience: "It's got to feel real." This should not be construed as merely an episode of positive, subjective feelings, but as an unmistakable engagement with the numinous—the self-validating presence of God in the midst of his gathered people. This does not replace the primacy of Scripture, but it is viewed as an essential companion.

Daniel Harrell

I have always questioned the concept of "church service." The word "service," as used within this phrase, can be traced back to its Latin origins of the medieval age involving three possible Latin nouns:

- *Beneficium*—originally a *benefice* was a gift of land (*precaria*) for life as a reward for services rendered.

The word comes from the Latin noun *beneficium*, meaning "benefit." A concept used by the Roman Catholic Church, it was abandoned by Protestantism (except in the Church of England).[1]

- *Munus*—a *munus* is a duty, gift, present, service, tribute, bribe, a public show (particularly of gladiators).[2]

- *Officium*—this implies dutiful or respectful action; attendance, service, duty; sense of duty, respect, courtesy; submission, allegiance.[3]

A "church *beneficium*"—a reward or benefit to the pastor or priest for services rendered—hardly fits our biblical understanding of what Christians do when we meet together within a local church. *Munus* and *officium* come closer to the iron-epoch culture's presentational church methodology in that they both carry the connotation of an exhibition or a "public show" or of attending to an event out of a "sense of duty" or obligation. These definitions betray a historic bias—specifically, that church leaders put on a public show that people attend out of a sense of duty and obligation.

This practice may have historic precedent, but is not a biblically informed concept of church or worship. In fact, the Bible tells us clearly how a church should be conducted. The apostle Paul was called by Christ to be a church planter. He established new churches within communities, appointed elders and then instructed church leadership on how he expected the church to function when its people came together. First Corinthians 14:26 and the greater context of this passage reveal some of Paul's instruction regarding what must and must not occur when the people of a local church come together:

> What then shall we say, brothers and sisters? When you come together, *each of you* has a hymn, or a word of instruction, a revelation, a tongue or an interpretation. Everything must be done so that the church may be built up.

A Pauline church never intended gatherings to be passive shows conducted by the elders, apostles, evangelists, pastors or teachers.

Paul's expectation of what should happen when church members come together involves individual *contribution* and *collaboration* whereby some church members use their unique gift sets to provide teaching, sing psalms of worship, speak in tongues and interpret or give prophetic revelations. Please note that Paul uses the all-inclusive phrase "each of you." There are no exceptions to the spiritual responsibility of personal contribution.

A Pauline church *never* intended gatherings to be passive shows conducted by the elders, apostles, evangelists, pastors or teachers. While Paul did advocate spiritual authority within each church in the form of elders, his charge to elders was to shepherd the church and, in some cases, to teach. Never once do we find an example in the Old or New Testament of a leader *performing* (as if pastors are mere actors on a stage) a church service. Rather than use the term "church service," Paul perceives of church membership as coming together in a manner in which each person contributes to the welfare of others out of their unique giftedness.

Clay-epoch young adults really resonate with the apostle Paul's directive that we should "come together" and that each one should contribute. But in most cases their experience of establishment church does not value their contribution. They feel that there are vitally important elements within our corporate worship gathering that seem to be missing. Chris Dorn, editor of *Reformed Review*, addresses this very issue:

> To the Emergents the truths of scripture do not express themselves only or even primarily in a set of doctrinal statements. This does not mean the neglect of the study of scripture. Nor does it mean the exclusion of it from corporate worship. But the truths of scripture are not only to be verbalized. They are to be embodied in spiritual disciplines and rituals, and, most importantly, in relationships and in service of the "other" that the former foster and sustain. This embodied and communal faith is what Christianity in the modern era lost; *the postmodern critique has opened up a conceptual space in which Emergents can reclaim these lost dimensions of the Christian faith.*[4]

In an attempt to "reclaim these lost dimensions of the Christian faith," some have experimented with forms and rituals from the medieval church era. While I can appreciate "smells and bells" vintage values (the use of incense censers and bells during worship and prayer in some high-church traditions), as stated earlier, I do not believe that the church can "emerge" into the present and future by regressing into its past.

Worship incarnate is a holistic immersion of our life in Christ.
Such a baptism cannot separate secular from sacred
or worship from mission.

The noble goal of such forms and ritual, however, is to help construct a worship environment that is far more *incarnate* than iron-epoch presentational church services permit. Christ incarnate is God in flesh. Similarly, worship incarnate is a holistic immersion of our life in Christ. Such a baptism cannot separate secular from sacred or worship from mission. The clay-epoch culture believes that corporate worship need not occur only at a large organization's campus or be an experience separated from personal application and practical ministry. To them iron-epoch church services feel artificial, like a virtual reality devoid of authenticity. The clay-epoch culture resists attempts to compartmentalize its faith and practice. Rather, clay-epoch worshipers prefer to integrate their worship expression into every facet of their lives.

These social and spiritual values have led people of the clay-epoch culture to de-emphasize church membership, denominational affiliation and even formalized church programming. They have rediscovered the global potential and affinity afforded by the "holy catholic church" (see the Apostle's Creed; the term "catholic" is derived from the Greek adjective καθολικός/*katholikos*, meaning "whole" or "complete"). In the same way that an Internet user logs on to the Internet and becomes one of billions of Internet nodes that comprise a whole, so young adults perceive their life in Christ. Listen to the personal manifesto of Rad Zdero, Canadian author and simple-church advocate:

> For too long, we Christians have identified ourselves with man-made institutions, especially Catholic, Orthodox, Anglican, and Protestant. But, the tide is turning! We now declare that Christianity is best lived out by getting back to the apostolic heritage of the New Testament in both faith and practice, function and form (1 Cor. 11:2, 14:36–38; 2 Thess. 2:15). . . . For too long, we Christians have engaged the world in "religious" ways, placing a wedge between body and spirit, sacred and secular, church and world, Great Commandment and Great Commission, loving God and loving people. But, the tide is turning! We now declare a grassroots Christianity that engages the world with the great news of Christ in a relevant way that can transform entire neighborhoods, cities, and nations.[5]

The Bible should always inform how we who are in Christ should function in this fallen world as His ambassadors. When church practices deviated from Scripture in the past, godly leaders such as Luther, Calvin, Zwingli and others were right to take steps to "reform" the church. For the most part, our presentational church services, based upon tradition and the influence of television, are in need of reformation.

Reformation is needed not only because we have deviated from the Bible's description of how Christ's church is to function when we come together but also because the values of the clay-epoch culture—that of grassroots contribution and collaboration of members within a community—fit perfectly with Paul's direction for how people should function when they come together. People within the clay-epoch culture need to be involved in worship. They need to experience for themselves the reality of a living Christ and personally respond through service to others in order to make a difference in their world. So what might it look like for people to function together as a church in which members actively participate in the interactive dialogue that is both worship and ministry? Please let me share just a few examples of how some ministries have attempted to bridge this culture gap.

The Jesus Movement Model

I experienced one example of a "church serve-us" during the Jesus Movement era of the early 1970s. A renegade Christian Reformed church pastor decided he would leave his denomination and its hierarchical authoritative structures and plant a church that looked as close to the Pauline biblical model as possible. So Pastor Calvin Bergsma founded Maranatha Ministries.

This church was unlike any I had ever experienced. In fact, I remember the very first Sunday I visited. I stepped out of the car and was suddenly confronted with over thirty bikers on their Harleys racing into the parking lot—I honestly thought the church was under attack. But as the bikers parked their bikes, I noticed that they all carried large leather-bound and studded Bibles. Then they gave each other bear hugs before entering the Party Place, where the church rented facilities.

As I walked into the main room, I saw for the first time in my adolescent life a congregation that was comprised of Asian, black, Hispanic and white people. The Dutch Reformed church I had been raised in always had 100 percent white attendees. The band kicked in, and for the next hour and a half, the dynamic praise and intimate worship never stopped except when people randomly and entirely without planning walked to the platform to share how Christ was at work within their lives. These testimonies just fueled the fire of thanksgiving and praise all over again.

Then the pastor stood and began to teach. He worked his way through the message verse by verse, explaining and expounding upon the text in a fresh, practical manner that did not make use of what I called the God-voice (the deep throaty voices pastors used to use whenever they prayed or preached). The service lasted over three hours, and I felt as if I had been there only fifteen minutes. I was hooked!

Over several years of actively participating in this church, it became evident to me that Pastor Bergsma built the church upon the following values:

1. The pastor's job was to equip the elders to teach within the body; the pastor and elders were to hold

people and one another publicly accountable for doctrinal error.

2. The elders, along with the pastor, taught in rotation, with each leader providing the teaching on different Sundays.

3. The atmosphere of church gatherings fostered a real sense of freedom and expectation that enabled people within the congregation to come forward to share whenever they believed they were being prompted by the Holy Spirit. The elders publicly and gently corrected any doctrinal error that people might communicate.

4. Worship songs of the Jesus Movement era were typically Scripture put to music. The worship team intentionally paused after the congregation sang a song to provide an opportunity for congregation members to begin singing a new worship song— the band quickly found the key of the song that the congregation had already begun to sing and caught up with them.

5. The church style had to be culturally relevant.

The Maranatha church strategy was simple and infectious. The ministry attracted Christ followers rapidly, growing from around one hundred people when I first began attending to nearly five hundred by the time Pastor Calvin Bergsma died. Pastor Bergsma was a unique man with a unique passion for doing church according to biblical directives rather than by tradition. However, Pastor Bergsma's vision and methodology is only one possible interpretation among many of how to implement congregational collaboration and gift-based contribution into a church. I have since observed themes and variations of the Jesus Movement model in our present clay-epoch culture.

The Café Model

One large seeker-driven church began to migrate from presentational services by deconstructing their established theater model. Noting the cultural popularity of coffee shops around the country, this church dedicated large portions of their building to cafés of various sizes ranging from seating for about one hundred people to private seating for as few as four. Each café venue contained a size-appropriate video screen with the ability to pause and mute the real-time teaching and worship as needed, allowing café participants to discuss among themselves how to live out what they were watching. In addition, this ministry contracted with various coffee cafés throughout the city to remain open on Sunday mornings. The church provided each café with a large video screen and streamed the worship and teachings to the café attendees. Each public café was staffed with volunteer "pastors" and "evangelists" who sought to build relationships with the café attendees and discuss with them what was being communicated via the video screen.

The Tech-Smart Model

A trend among churches targeting people of the clay-epoch culture is the use of Twitter or some other more secure text-based community to enable a measure of dialogue to occur during the church teaching time. In this model it is common to see attendees using laptops, iPads and smartphones during the service. Church attendees are encouraged to post questions and interactions regarding the teaching in real time. A technical team intercepts the online questions and forwards some of the questions to the teaching pastor via his laptop, iPad or video monitor. This enables the teaching pastor to respond to the questions in real time, providing some measure of interactive dialogue.

The questions posted then become the basis for later online discussion hosted by the church leadership in which attendees can interact with the pastors and others participating in the discussion regarding how to live and apply what they are learning. Tools such as YouVersion, WebEx, GoToMeeting and others enable live conferencing whereby Christ followers can interact with each other and with church leadership to dig deeper into the spiritual struggle that people previously posted about online.

The "Bring Something to the Table" Model

One intriguing model that reaches back to the 1970s coffeehouses advocates restructuring multipurpose auditoriums from theater seating to seating around tables. In this model, people sit in table groups of approximately ten people. Water, coffee, cups and possibly some simple snacks are offered in the center of each table. Often there is a trained host and/or facilitator assigned to each table group. Unlike the "turn and greet" moment used in many churches, this structure makes it far easier for people to meet one another and truly begin to build authentic relationships. Some churches even provide a fellowship break of ten to fifteen minutes between the worship period and the teaching period. During the teaching, the pastor will stop his or her monologue at certain points and assign questions or issues for table members to discuss.

A more advanced form of this model provides daily study guides that are e-mailed to the church membership to help them prepare for the upcoming teaching time. People receiving the daily study guides are encouraged to post questions or comments regarding each day's topic to help inform the teaching pastor of issues or testimonies that may be incorporated within the upcoming Sunday teaching. Participants are also encouraged to "bring something to the table" on Sunday by being prepared to share insights, testimonies and the like with the people seated at their table. The goal is to emphasize a culture that values and promotes relational connections as well as personal contribution and collaboration.

The House-Church Model

In recent years, particularly within the church-planting world, there have been attempts to deconstruct the large-church concept into small house churches consisting of eight to twenty people. Often one pastor oversees multiple microcongregations in the manner of an itinerate pastor, who during the 1700–1800s commonly traveled from church to church. This model does indeed emphasize the contributions of its individual members, and the group dynamic also allows for inclusive collaboration.

The challenge, however, with the house-church model is that it can easily degenerate into an inward-focused social clique. Evangelistic growth may be limited since the house church can only grow to a maximum of twenty people or it will be subdivided, a process that people who may have grown close to one another typically seek to avoid.

Similarly, the house-church model can have difficulty generating enough organizational synergy so as to be inclusive of people possessing less relational temperaments, such as those whose temperaments are more task driven or mission focused. Yet in spite of the obstacles presented by the house-church model, many people are strong advocates of this ministry method.

The Interactive-Application Model

During one period of time, I had the opportunity to attend, many times, an intriguing church-inside-a-church model designed for young adults in their twenties. However, although targeted to young adults within the church, the interactive elements of the services attracted people of all ages. The singing time was progressive and artistic—one never really knew what to expect each Sunday. This creativity kept the corporate worship service fresh and surprising. The teaching time was an extended period of expository instruction with an honest focus upon real-life application. But the pinnacle of the service was the application time. Rather than excuse people out the back door to determine on their own how to apply what had been taught, church leadership integrated an extended period of personal application. Various stations were set up around the worship center for people to interact with and apply the teaching prayerfully within their life.

These application stations changed in number and purpose each week. For example, if the teaching had been on the gracious forgiveness available to us through Christ Jesus, there might have been one station with a large mirror on the wall on which people could write the sins they felt convicted of upon the mirror and then use a cloth and glass cleaner to wipe their sins away. Another station might have had a pot full of burning coals surrounded by burning incense depicting prayers reaching the Father as a "sweet smelling sacrifice"; people would write their prayers or confessions upon a piece of paper and then throw the paper into the flames. Still another station might have been allowed for people to meet with one another to confess their sins toward one another and to receive forgiveness and restored relationships in Christ. At each station people gifted in intercessory prayer were stationed to pray with those who requested prayer.

These services were powerful. The teachings and the worship of Christ became authentic in the moment because worshipers acted upon the Holy Spirit's prompting within the spirit of each Christ follower. This model is challenging in its creative demands, but in my personal experience, it is well worth the effort.

Reaching Out with Authenticity

These are only a few creative examples in which ministries seek to reform their structures and methodology so as to become inclusive of the clay-epoch cultural values. Each church has unique qualities, so each solution may also be unique. However, if a church is presently an iron-epoch service style, I suggest that a separate "outreach" ministry be formed either as a church-within-a-church strategy or at an off-campus location in a warehouse or other commercial property. This strategy will provide the necessary freedom to experiment and discover which strategies will work best in a particular community context.

Although we have examined several models of interactive teaching and worship, it is not so that church leaders reading this book will pick one and try to artificially implement it. What the people of the clay-epoch culture value more than anything is authenticity. Their technical society is replete with virtual reality, so when it comes to their faith life, they long for authentic reality. Instead, I challenge pastoral leaders to prayerfully develop a culture of worship and teaching that is highly personal, vulnerable and, most of all, authentic.

As church leaders, we should peel away the "performer" in our worship and teaching pastors. We should let the real person beneath the performing persona be revealed. Reveal what it looks like to really love and worship Christ. Reveal what it looks like to wrestle with the Holy Spirit in prayer. Reveal what faith looks like when Bible promises don't seem to make sense and it feels as if God has abandoned His child. Every Christ follower has been there. Every Christ follower lives the daily struggle that is faith.

Out of this position of vulnerability, in which the pastor does not have the perfect sermon, the perfect solutions or the perfect prayers, we should invite people into honest dialogue. That dialogue will look different from church to church. The dialogue will transform how we do church and, more importantly, how we live together as Christ's church. Vulnerability, authenticity and a maturing value of interactive dialogue will help our churches begin to close the culture gap that in most American churches today is widening rapidly.

7

Evangelism in the Internet-Influenced Church

The Church exists for nothing else but to draw men into Christ, to make them little Christs. If they are not doing that, all the cathedrals, clergy, missions, sermons, even the Bible itself, are simply a waste of time. God became Man for no other purpose.

C. S. Lewis

The ministry of evangelist is listed in Ephesians 4:11 alongside that of pastor and teacher as being a crucial role in helping equip people for the work of ministry service. In fact, without the ministry of evangelism—the first mission directive of the church that we identified in chapter 5—the spiritual formation process within the lives of people would likely not begin. The apostle Paul tells us in Romans 10,

How, then, can they call on the one they have not believed
in? And how can they believe in the one of whom they
have not heard? And how can they hear without someone
preaching to them? And how can they preach unless they
are sent? As it is written: "How beautiful are the feet of
those who bring good news!" (10:14–15)

The word "preach" or "preaching" occurs 123 times in
the New Testament. One hundred twenty-one times the
word clearly infers public proclamation of the good news
among nonbelievers. The apostle Paul's discourse on Mars
Hill is an excellent example of preaching.

Preaching is not the same as teaching, a truth largely
misunderstood within many of our present-day presentational churches. The Great Commission calls us to make
disciples through teaching, not preaching. From a biblical
perspective preaching is *proclamational*, while teaching is
incarnational—or put more simply, in preaching we communicate a predefined message called the gospel of Jesus
Christ, the good news; in teaching we live out the gospel of
Jesus Christ and all that He has commanded us before others who are seeking to learn what a fully devoted follower
of Christ looks like.

Through teaching we who are in Christ *become* more like
Christ as His Spirit lives in us, guides and directs us, teaches
us through the Word and transforms us continuously to live
and serve Christ as our Lord. But this spiritual-formation
process begins through preaching, when the good news is
first proclaimed to us. It is the Holy Spirit who authors
our faith, enabling us first to accept and receive eternal

redemption through the person and work of Jesus Christ and then to submit to the Spirit's continual sanctification within our lives. A Christ follower assists in this incredible spiritual process simply by preaching and teaching through his or her life.

In many biblical examples preaching is not particularly relational, as the message was communicated to large groups typically as a monologue. However, in every biblical example I can find, teaching is always relational, as people invited others into their homes to "break bread" with one another and to learn from one of the apostles or one of the appointed house/synagogue elders or through the iron-sharpening-iron process of interpersonal instruction. The distinction between preaching as proclamation and teaching as incarnation cannot be overstressed. When pastors misunderstand this distinction, they will preach every Sunday to believers, resulting in very little evangelistic success, while ignoring essential incarnational teaching that would be able to help Christ followers develop into mature disciples.

The television-influenced church of the latten iron-epoch culture tends to prefer preaching over relational teaching. Through the various mediums of their day—radio, television, movies, the church pulpit, tent revivals, mass-arena evangelistic events typified by Billy Graham crusades or the Promise Keepers movement of the 1990s—the television-culture church has been effective at producing presentational events and programs that proclaim the gospel message.

Throughout the 1980s and '90s and even to some extent today, seeker-driven and seeker-sensitive ministry strategies have restructured church services throughout the United States. This generation commonly placed an emphasis upon proclaiming the gospel message and challenging seekers to make a decision for Christ. While this methodology can still work today, because the Holy Spirit is the One who does the real work when the gospel is proclaimed, evangelism in the clay-epoch culture is more commonly a process that supports people as their faith develops in Jesus Christ over time and through interpersonal experiences.

The Holy Spirit has definitely used simple tools such as *The Four Spiritual Laws* and the *Romans Road*. However, today's clay-epoch culture is resistant to prepackaged solutions that promise them the world with little personal cost or investment. They intuitively discern that there is more to one's spiritual journey than formula Christianity.

People who comprise the clay-epoch culture typically share a socially indoctrinated belief that there may be many paths to God and that all truth is relative to one's experience. As a result, spiritual exploration takes people considerable time and effort before they can be personally convinced of the truth and exclusivity of faith in Jesus Christ. This ongoing process of faith development is often referred to as spiritual formation, a nomenclature I find helpful to remind me that while the evangelistic message can result in instant conversion experiences, more commonly the Holy Spirit works upon the hearers' hearts over time as they are exposed to both biblical teaching and the incarnational faith life of their rabbi-teachers.

Incarnational teaching is risky. It demands that the rabbi-teacher be honest and vulnerable about his or her own relationship with Jesus Christ. It is my experience that our human egos prefer to preach rather than teach, because in preaching we can portray ourselves to the crowd as authoritative leaders who have the answers to life in Christ. Incarnational teaching, however, requires the rabbi-teacher to convey what he or she has learned—and is currently learning—as he or she personally follows Christ through both perceived failures and successes.

We are all fallible sinful humans. When we portray ourselves as anything but fallible faith followers of Jesus Christ who owe Him all that we are becoming—even the faith to believe that from moment to moment Christ alone is perfecting us by His Spirit and does so for His glory alone—we deceive ourselves and in our pride seek to steal some of the Holy Spirit's glory for ourselves. Evangelism and disciple making within the clay-epoch culture happens most effectively as Christ-followers follow, speak and serve in humility. When in humility we emphasize what we are created for—the glorification of Christ and His transformative work within our own lives—and reject the moralistic platitudes that incite the world to label Christ followers as hypocrites, we leave room for the Holy Spirit to work through His gentle and loving patience to draw the unbeliever unto Himself.

Sadly, most churches today do not practice intentional biblical spiritual formation principles. Over the years I have asked church leaders and elder boards a troubling question:

"What does a fully devoted follower of Christ look like, and how do we support an individual's spiritual development from seeker to mature Christ follower?" Most church leaders cannot agree upon what a fully devoted follower of Christ looks like, let alone define a methodology of how to help such individuals grow into spiritual maturity.

Disciple making is the prime mission of Christ's church. If church leaders do not know how to support the disciple-making process, then it should be of no surprise to us that the laity no longer trusts spiritual leaders to help them grow spiritually. As a result, the clay-realm culture intuitively discerns that there is something wrong with the form of Christianity that we espouse.

On the blog *Q: Ideas for the Common Good*, David Kinnaman observes,

> Like a corrupted computer file or a bad photocopy, Christianity, they say, is no longer in pure form, and so they reject it. One-quarter of outsiders say that their foremost perception of Christianity is that the faith has changed for the worse. It has gotten off track and is not what Christ intended. Modern-day Christianity no longer seems Christian.

Kinnaman continues to site statistics regarding how young people ages 16–29 view the present expressions of Christianity:

- Antihomosexual, 91 percent
- Judgmental, 87 percent
- Hypocritical, 85 percent

- Sheltered (old-fashioned, out of touch with reality), 78 percent

- Too political, 75 percent

- Proselytizers (insensitive to others, not genuine), 70 percent[1]

Effective evangelists within the clay realm will speak less about God's declaration of homosexuality as a sin and more about the evangelist's personal struggles with all types of sexual sin because we are all fallen and broken people for whom Christ offers forgiveness and liberation.

Effective evangelists in the clay-realm will not judge others; they will first judge themselves and admit to others their total depravity and inability to change themselves.

I think you get the point.

At its core clay-realm evangelism demands of the evangelist raw honesty expressed in true humility. Gone are the days of simply asking a stranger, "Do you know where you would go if you died today?" Too many anti-Christian preconceptions are now stacked against us for such simple devices to be effective.

Honestly, we (I include myself) must take responsibility for our role in helping society form these preconceptions. We church leaders have been far too concerned with our image, our leadership skills and the size of our churches. Christianity has become the victim of a television-influenced church culture that screams in words and imagery, "Success like ours can be yours if you would only choose to follow Christ the way we follow Christ."

Recently a staffer from a mega seeker church resigned a position that he had held there for a good number of years. He was clearly hurting. I asked him if he would be willing to share with me what had happened to bring him to ultimately resign. He shared with me that the lead pastor had established a culture in which no staffer was ever allowed to ask for help. The lead pastor believed that the church hired only the best and most qualified spiritual leaders and so, as examples to the congregation, they were never permitted to show weakness. This staffer could no longer manage the internal and external stresses he was being forced to deal with in an iron-culture presentational church in which a perfected image presented to the congregation was the highest value.

This man knew his own weaknesses and personal struggles. I congratulated him for having the integrity to no longer project a lie of Christian perfectionism in the name of Christ. In reality, confided this ex-staffer to me, the perfect image that staff members were expected to project actually alienated the staff from the seekers they were supposedly working to reach, because those same seekers often felt that they would never measure up to such standards.

Not too long ago a megachurch leader reported to me that the church's lead pastor had had an affair with a woman in the church. The lead pastor was the outward image of the "perfect Christian leader." He was a gifted positive motivator and speaker. He was physically fit and attractive. He projected an air of excellence and professionalism. Sadly, when the affair became public, the pastor distanced himself from the woman (who also had a husband and children). As a result of her shame and feelings of rejection, she committed suicide. The church quietly dismissed the pastor who within months was hired to be the lead pastor of another megachurch in another state.

So how does the clay realm consequently view the values of the television-influenced church? Image is idolatry. Perfection is but a liar's facade. Organizations are political entities solely concerned with their own self-subsistence. The clay realm might have been willing to put up with the fog of politics, facades and even possibly the idolatry of image had the television-influenced church made any attempt to truly "make disciples," but sadly this prime directive from Jesus Christ our Lord has been largely neglected.

A dangerous cycle has emerged: most churches fail to make an intentional effort to invest in, track and support their people's personal spiritual formation, resulting in a justifiable skepticism among people who comprise the clay-epoch culture of the local church's ability to help them develop spiritually.

Spiritual formation, or as some prefer to call it, disciple making, should be the primary task of the local church. Unfortunately, studies reveal that most churches do not consider this vital process within people's lives worthy of tracking. George Barna, in his April 2005 Perspectives letter entitled "New Direction," makes an astounding observation:

The most discouraging study we ever conducted was one in which we attempted to identify churches in the U.S. that consistently and intelligently evaluate life transformation among the people to whom they minister. We found that very few churches—emphasis on very—measure anything beyond attendance, donations, square footage, number of programs and size of staff. None of that necessarily reflects life transformation.[2]

A dangerous cycle has emerged: most churches fail to make an intentional effort to invest in, track and support their people's personal spiritual formation, resulting in a justifiable skepticism among people who comprise the clay-epoch culture of the local church's ability to help them develop spiritually. Increasingly, Internet-influenced people no longer look to the local church for their spiritual formation needs. Clearly, from their perspective the established church is broken. Rather, the clay-epoch culture now gathers information via the Internet at a pace that was never before possible. This culture is defined by its ability to self-educate. In assessing the emerging Internet influences upon our culture, the Pew Internet and American Life Project asserts,

> Hyperlinks subvert hierarchy. The Net will wear away institutions that have forgotten how to sound human and how to engage in conversation. . . . Enabled by information technologies, the pace of learning in the next decade will increasingly be set by student choices. In ten years, most students will spend at least part of their "school days" in virtual classes, grouped online with others who share their interests, mastery, and skills.[3]

These realities have led to a present and unfolding culture that holds a profound disenchantment with "out-of-touch" preachers and teachers. Young adults no longer feel a need for a personal rabbi-teacher within their lives. Students are able to gather up-to-date information quickly and challenge their instructors even as instructors espouse out-of-date information in an out-of-date manner as they have for most of their careers.

People of the clay-epoch culture bring these learning preferences into their local congregations and into their personal spiritual formation process. How has the American church responded? In most cases adult Christian education is nonexistent. The old paradigms of Sunday school and catechism have proven largely irrelevant to people of the clay-epoch culture, yet most churches have not replaced these paradigms with new culturally relevant incarnational strategies. Sadly, as traditional discipleship programs decline, pastors commonly respond to this problem by blaming their people for being "too busy" or "uninterested" in spiritual things.

The "net" result is that in an age of communication and information technology, biblical literacy is at an historic low. Our church leaders are doing little to facilitate spiritual formation in the lives of their followers, so the followers are ill-equipped to help facilitate spiritual formation in the lives of their peers. The disciple-making life cycle is now entirely broken.

But we must have faith. God always reserves for Himself a remnant of faithful Christ followers whom

He will use to ensure that His kingdom plan reaches culmination.

In his graduate thesis David Eikenberry asked churches and youth pastors in West Michigan (a highly churched community of the Dutch Reformed tradition) to administer a simple biblical literacy survey to parishioners. "The scores were just atrocious," he said. "I don't expect those outside Christianity to know the Christian book, but I do think the people of the Book should be familiar with it?"[4]

Is it any wonder that the people of the clay-epoch culture have become cynical toward spiritual authority figures? From their perspective just because a figurehead who appears to be building his own kingdom tells people to follow Christ, that is no reason in the minds of many to do so. In fact, *telling* people of the clay-epoch culture to do anything will likely result in rebellious rejection. The era of "proclaim it, name it and claim it"—dominant themes espoused by televangelists of the previous era—is now passé. We must *show* today's culture how to follow Christ, first earning that right by demonstrating a sincere, humble, authentic and transparent faith relationship with God.

The clay-epoch era prefers a process of personal spiritual facilitation. A spiritual facilitator helps individuals discover biblical information and supports the individual's testing of that information within his or her own search for God. In essence, people of the clay-epoch culture are challenging the church to do far less talk about God. Rather, they desire assistance interacting with God. They crave what Romans hat great theological apex of the New Testament, speaks about when it says we are to live by the Spirit or put to death our sin issues by the Spirit. Sadly, the presentational church medium is ill-equipped to walk people through this highly experiential and personalized process that occurs within the life of every Christ follower.

If we think about it, personal spiritual interaction has been a value of all previous generations. In fact, it is a core desire within every human heart, ordained within us at creation, modeled for us when God walked and talked with Adam in the garden. Who would not rather walk and talk with God than study facts and information about Him? Similarly, the emerging generations rightfully expect of Christ's church that we will help them personally meet with God. Their desire to learn more about Him biblically flows naturally from this authentic relationship of living by the Spirit.

Sermons such as "three easy steps to grow in Christ" or "five ways to improve your marriage this week" are simplistic and lacking in authenticity. People of the clay-epoch culture innately discern that the way of the cross will not be easy. When church leaders try to make the Christ life sound easy, as if they have broken the magical Bible code, they only alienate the young adults they are trying to reach.

One positive step some churches have made to overcome evangelistic deficiencies is to hire staff to serve as full-time Internet ambassadors or Internet evangelists. Through the use of social networks, live video conferencing and live-help chat rooms, utilized commonly by secular businesses for customer support, Internet evangelists provide real-time relational and interactive support for people exploring faith in Jesus Christ.

Personal crisis often drives people to seek God's help and support in their lives. Traditional church staff structures and office hours do not provide the same measure of real-time support that Internet interactions provide. In addition, as I addressed previously, Internet interactions often provide a powerful sense of intimacy at a distance; people become very real and vulnerable quickly when online. The Internet provides a type of emotional veneer that feels less risky than being face to face with church pastors and staff. As a result, Internet evangelists are able to make significant kingdom advances on a global scale as never before possible.

I recognize that a number of readers are church pastors and staff who currently serve in a television-inspired iron-epoch church, and many are trying to better understand the impact that the influence of the Internet is having upon how to do church. For these readers I feel a need to stress that having a quality church website does not count as Internet evangelism. Nor does hosting a blog with articles that address church programming and events. And again, streaming monologue sermons online does not count as Internet evangelism. True Internet evangelism strategies within the clay-epoch era must contain the following elements as a minimum in order to legitimately be labeled Internet evangelism:

1. *Relational interaction.* "Be completely humble and gentle; be patient, bearing with one another in love" (Eph. 4:2).

2. *Real-time response.* "We sent Timothy, who is our brother and co-worker in God's service in spreading the gospel of Christ, to strengthen and encourage you in your faith" (1 Thess. 3:2).

3. *A sensitive listening ear.* "A false witness will perish, but a careful listener will testify successfully" (Prov. 21:28).

4. *Willingness to support online seekers over an extended period of time.* "Be completely humble and gentle; be patient, bearing with one another in love" (Eph. 4:2).

These are the same principles that ministry leaders advocate when working with face-to-face evangelistic relationships. The only real difference is that Internet evangelism makes use of a virtual office as compared to a pastor's study.

Gordon Marcy, in his April 23, 2012, *Church Central* article "Has Internet Evangelism Reached the Tipping Point?" makes the following observations:

> Using the Internet for evangelism and discipleship had reached the tipping point for this congregation. The church, like many others today, has empirical evidence that people are being reached online. Lives are being impacted by the gospel.
>
> Online missionaries get to experience that pretty quickly. Online connections with seekers seem to get "very deep, very fast," even through email. It's surprising, really.

And additionally,

> Christians doing ministry online have the awesome
> privilege of making themselves available to individuals
> at the precise moment of need. We can't do everything,
> of course. And we're not in physical touch. But, we can
> answer their biblical and personal questions. We can dis-
> cuss scripture. We can pray that God will connect them
> to a local church. We can show genuine compassion.[5]

Internet Evangelism Day is an Internet organization that
promotes an annual day to commemorate the value of Internet evangelism. The 2014 Internet Evangelism Day is on
Sunday, June 1. In their planning guide, this ministry challenges pastors to rethink their communication paradigm:

> We must understand the nature of social networking to use
> it effectively. If we think of it as one-way publicity, we will
> be ineffective and irritating. Social networking is people
> and two-way relationships. Think "cafe," not "pulpit."[6]

Our television-inspired church paradigm has significantly altered many pastors' concept of relational ministry
interactions. Pastors today commonly have a rule that they
will meet with individuals on a limited basis, generally once
or at most three times. I do not believe that this is the "café"
experience the Internet evangelism website has in mind.
Relationships must be sincere and authentic. Authentic relationships take time. In the clay-epoch era, if pastors feel
that they are too busy to invest in sincere relationships with
people at their initial stages of spiritual formation, then, in
essence, these pastors have simply decided that they are too

busy to do evangelism. It is for this reason that aggressive church ministries hire full-time staff members to build an extended support network for online evangelistic ministry. Is the financial investment into a dedicated staff member worthwhile? That one staff member will likely reach more people in one year for Christ than a brick-and-mortar church will.

Another hurdle for many television-influenced pastors to overcome is the realization that many of the people reached for Christ via an Internet evangelism ministry will never step foot inside their church buildings. In the clay-epoch culture pastors must think both locally and globally ("glocally"). We must value building Christ's kingdom around the world versus building our own little kingdoms on the corner of Fifth and Main Streets.

While most pastors I have met will intellectually affirm this challenge, their actions often betray alternate priorities. The television-influenced church typically judges success by how many people are in the seats rather than by how many disciples have been made. I have often heard pastoral leaders assert, "People count—that's why we count people." This may sound good, but do people really count if we have an auditorium full of people but have no idea how those hundreds or thousands of people are progressing spiritually? If we truly cared about people's spiritual welfare, should we not care enough to intentionally invest into their spiritual development?

This is exactly the point of contention that young adults of the clay epoch have with iron-epoch churches.

Presentational ministry methodology almost always substitutes a performance in place of authentic relational ministry. What is the resulting attitude among people of the clay epoch? "If church leaders do not care enough to get to know me, to know my struggles and share my pain, then I don't care enough to attend their Sunday performances." This is the nature and intensity of the cultural divide that the television-inspired church must learn to bridge. We cannot retain our old ministry strategies and merely modify them slightly to meet the needs of today's young people. Nowhere is this cultural divide more apparent than when we try to reach the people of the clay-epoch culture for Jesus Christ.

8

Discipleship in the
Internet-Influenced Church

*Christianity without discipleship is always
Christianity without Christ.*

Dietrich Bonhoeffer

iscicple making, our second mission directive, involves much more than simply introducing people
to Christ. Disciple making is a lifelong process of
cooperating with the work of the Holy Spirit to help mold
the nature, character and mission of an individual as he or
she becomes more and more like his or her Rabbi-Teacher.
Jesus, our lead Rabbi-Teacher, charged His disciples with
one primary mission, found in Matthew 28:

> Then Jesus came to them and said, "All authority in
> heaven and on earth has been given to me. Therefore go
> and make disciples of all nations, baptizing them in the

name of the Father and of the Son and of the Holy Spirit, and teaching them to obey everything I have commanded you. And surely I am with you always, to the very end of the age. (Matt. 28:18–20)

I like to refer to what is commonly known as the Great Commission as the "Great Co-mission," because all Christ followers for all generations are called to join with Christ in the pursuit of this great mission. Furthermore, Christ Himself promises to join us in the pursuit of this mission, even to the end of the age. The disciple-making mandate carries with it two clear instructions: (1) we are to baptize, and (2) we are to teach.

While the Internet may become a very useful medium for extending many ministry responsibilities, it will never replace the local church.

These instructions present an obstacle to our present Internet-influenced culture regarding disciple making. We can easily teach online. In fact, it can be argued that we can teach far more effectively online than we can teach offline. However, no matter how hard I might try, I cannot construe a practical means of baptizing someone over the Internet. So what does this tell us about Internet-based discipleship? It is limited. While the Internet may become a very useful medium for extending many ministry responsibilities, it will never replace the local church.

In the late 1990s there were Internet ministry prophets

suggesting to the church that someday people would no longer go to a brick-and-mortar facility to attend church but would simply log in online. These prophets would speak of the cyberchurch, or the e-church, replacing the local church entirely. I do not believe that this prognostication is valid. I am convinced that the e-church will not replace the local church. Rather, there will be a convergence of the e-church with the reality church that will transform the global Internet community and the local church alike.

The local congregation will continue to do what it does best. However, it will no longer see itself as an isolated entity unto itself. The local church will be transformed from seeking to build its own little kingdom in its niche of the world (the iron-epoch model) to having a responsibility to network with ministries across the globe, supporting and mentoring disciples even a continent away and helping them to find or establish a local community of faith. Likewise, church planting, along with the nurture and support of church-plant pastors online, will likely expand at an unprecedented pace. I believe this vision of the future to be valid because it is already happening today.

In 2007 Rick Warren, pastor of Saddleback Church and author of *The Purpose Driven Church* and *The Purpose Driven Life*, was interviewed by Fox News Network. In that interview Pastor Warren conveyed how the vast sums of money that were generated by the sale of his book, *The Purpose Driven Life*, were now enabling him to live on 10 percent of his income and invest 90 percent into ministry. In particular Rick and his wife were activists serving

Africa in an effort to overcome the AIDS epidemic. In a recent visit to Africa, he was introduced to a man in a small impoverished village who served as the village pastor. This man had no formal education. However, once each week he traveled into the local city to visit a cybercafé. At the cybercafé each week this man downloaded the podcast (Internet broadcast) of Rick Warren's weekly message, memorized it and then went home and recounted the teaching to his small congregation.[1] This is only one example of how church planting and leadership training are evolving in unprecedented ways.

Discipleship Goes Global

The clay-epoch culture perceives itself as holding membership in a global community. Shared geography is no longer the basis for social connections. Rather, shared passions, interests and missions coalesce people who were once entirely unrelated into cohesive social subgroups. Gary Kreps, chair of communication at George Mason University, writes, "Increased access to information about different people will enhance our understanding of different cultures and promote greater intercultural sensitivity. . . . People will recognize similarities in values and goals and use these shared values as a basis for coordination and cooperation."[2]

Online social networking enables young adults to interact with people across the globe. Online information networks (RSS/XML, blog news feeds and wikis) enable young adults to be constantly aware of global challenges. The ease of global travel enables people to join with short-term mission teams to help address global crisis and challenges. People of the clay-epoch culture firmly believe that they possess real potential for global impact. Let me repeat this: *people of the clay-epoch culture firmly believe that they possess real potential for global impact.* Ministry organizations that empower and equip their people to "go into all the world"—both virtually and physically—will likely thrive in the years to come. Similarly, those organizations and systems that focus predominantly upon their local community will likely diminish.

Discipleship via Social Networks

Disciple making as a process is really no different in the clay-epoch culture than in other cultures with the sole exception being that Internet social networking enables relationships to extend beyond borders and cultures. Within the context of these relationships, true teaching, leadership training and emotional and spiritual nurture takes place. For example, one of our international ministry clients (which desires to remain anonymous due to the nature of its ministry) uses our secure online training environments (eChurchNetwork.net) to train and support the development of native house-church pastors within China.

Paul D. Watson of the blog *Reaching the Online Generation* writes in his September 1, 2010 post,

> Most of the issues facing churches and ministries these days are not technology issues. They are discipleship issues. Technology is just a spotlight, a magnifying glass, revealing overlooked or hidden problems with discipleship in the Western church and its progeny. If we don't address

the discipleship issues, we will create another generation of predominately shallow and infertile Christians . . . and we will have a great time playing with our websites and iPads in the process.[3]

Paul gets it! The issue is not technology. The issue before us is disciple making and the refusal of the American church to invest itself into the time-consuming and relationally challenging work that is disciple making. When the American church adopted a television-influenced ministry paradigm—one that values presentational strategies—it simultaneously began to deemphasize the art of relational disciple making. So much time, money and human resources were invested into producing the Sunday productions and programs that people had little energy or time for more relational ministry pursuits.

David Kueker, in chapter 1 of his doctoral thesis on disciple making, concurs:

> Perhaps we do not know how to make disciples. The general response of clergy to the question of how one makes disciples is that "if people come to worship they eventually become disciples." This view indicates disciple-making as an event, an accidental result due to unknown causes, a mysterious act of God, rather than an intentional process. Churches are busy with many activities that may be very spiritually satisfying but do not make disciples that can be counted; these religious activities rarely interest and involve non-Christians. Based on what churches actually do, the common belief is that proclamation makes disciples, that church buildings make disciples, that worship makes

disciples, that advertising makes disciples, that an attractive church bulletin makes disciples, that a busy church program makes disciples, that church committees make disciples and that acts of mercy, justice and community service make disciples. The numbers indicate that these practices do not make disciples. Working harder at what does not work and avoiding opportunities to study what does work allows systems to remain the same.[4]

The consequence of the television-influenced church investing its resources into anything and everything short of rabbi-disciple relational teaching strategies is that now an entire generation is largely biblically illiterate. They have nearly no practical idea of what reproductive disciple making looks like. After all, it is difficult for most people to give to others something that they have not themselves received.

This reality in part contributes to the perception among people of the clay-epoch culture that something is wrong with our current expression of church. For many this feeling is intangible, something they cannot quite put their finger on. As a result, young Christ followers retrace church history seeking to recapture what may have been lost. Still others seek to recapture a sense of mission by investing their time in social justice and social action. All these and many other practices are mere attempts, in my opinion, to rediscover the life-changing vitality that Christians once experienced as disciples of Christ who cooperated with the work of the Spirit of Christ to make disciples.

The Internet-influenced church, using wise Internet social-networking strategies, reasserts itself not as a faceless institution but as a body of relational Christian leaders who are eager to spend time listening and responding to people's struggles and needs. There is an old leadership principle that applies to this point: "People must know how much you care before they will care how much you know." The Judaic culture in the time of Jesus understood this. The highest honor that one could receive was to be called to be a disciple of a rabbi. Beth HaDerech, a Messianic Christian, describes the experience:

> When the rabbi believed that you were call(ed) by HaShem to be his talmid (student), he would say, "*Lech Acharai*—come, follow me." And you would leave your family. You would leave your family compound. You would leave your village. You would leave the local synagogue where you had been studying. You would leave everything and you would follow that rabbi. You would become a talmid, a disciple, a student. You would give your life to being exactly like that rabbi. And you would follow him everywhere."[5]

The people of the clay epoch are hungry for spiritual leaders to call them, to hear them say *Lech Acharai*, to be taught by them to obey all that Christ has commanded. I believe they want to follow a rabbi daily and learn from them how to best love their Lord and minister in His name. However, unlike when Jesus called His disciples with little apparent previous relationship, today's young adults need spiritual leaders to first prove themselves to be authentic before they will dare entrust their spiritual welfare into a rabbi's care. The television-influenced church has displayed many hypocritical and sinful leaders who have been outed by the news media (Jimmy Swaggart, Jim Baker, Peter Popoff and others) and tarnished the reputation of Christianity almost beyond repair.

People of the clay-epoch culture are media savvy. They know of too many fallen pastors, too many showmen and far too much deceit and manipulation involving money scams in the name of Christ. This mental image creates an almost impassable chasm that separates the people of the clay-epoch culture from the religious culture of the iron-epoch church. Today's generation is fed up with fraud. For young adults of the clay-epoch culture, most everything associated with the present day's expression of church sounds and looks like the spam sitting in their e-mail inbox.

Complicating matters further, 72 percent of young African-American adults within the clay-epoch culture have been raised in broken homes or single-parent homes.[6] Approximately 40 percent of Caucasians were raised in single-parent homes.[7] While I am confident that some of these home situations were truly loving and nurturing, as a whole, young adults are skeptical of true love and commitment even being possible. Furthermore, their perception of a generational gap, which they believe makes the opposing generations perceive the world quite differently from one another, is now worse than it was in the height of the 1960s hippie era:

A survey conducted in February 2009 found that Americans are just as likely now as they were during the turbulent 1960s to say there is a generation gap between young and old. In the 2009 survey, 79% said there is a major difference in the point of view of younger people and older people today; 74% said the same in 1969.[8]

Christ's church must confront this culture's distrust of authority figures by demonstrating that the individual is more important than the establishment's "little-k kingdom" church, that the individual's pain points are validated through sincere listening and support and that ministry leaders can be trusted as they practice what they preach and invest their teachings personally into the life of the clay-epoch individual. It is the responsibility of all Christ followers, and especially church leaders, to demonstrate Christ's love in both word and deed. This kind of love is willing to make a commitment to relationship; it inspires us to invest our lives into the lives of others—letting people walk with us daily as we serve as their rabbi-teacher. In all honesty, at best we can humbly serve as assistant rabbis, or, as Jesus put it, under-shepherds (see 1 Pet. 5:1–4), for our one true Rabbi is Jesus Christ who teaches all of us daily by the power of His Spirit and through His Word. Our relationships should be formed in and through and around the person of Jesus Christ. It is Christ's love, in the words of the apostle Paul, that should compel us to serve in His name (see 2 Cor. 5:14). Bottom line: pastors need to get off stage, out of the office and into the lives of the people who will comprise the Internet-influenced church.

Discipleship via E-Learning

What could discipleship and chess ever hold in common? Well, let me explain. My son, a chess enthusiast, is listed among the top fifty chess players in the nation for his age category. One of his favorite learning activities occurs live online twice a week. Twice a week, at a set time, a chess master broadcasts a live chess game. Students from around the world are able to log into the program and observe the broadcast. However, they are also able to interact with the chess master by texting in comments and suggestions in real time. The chess master responds verbally to the many messages being received.

I hope that you can truly perceive the magnitude of this instructional scenario: a chess master is literally playing a game of chess against all the students around the world who are logged into the system in real time. The chess master makes a move and then verbally invites the students to text in what they believe would be the wisest next move. The chess master discusses the pros and cons of the various recommended moves. Based upon majority opinion, the chess master not only moves the piece accordingly but then instructs the students as to the strengths and weaknesses of that move as well as possible variations of it.

This program has taken an instructional experience that for over two thousand years has occurred between a single coach and a few students and implemented that training experience on a global scale. Such is the potential of e-learning.

Relational e-learning is a disciple-making medium that television-inspired churches have either ignored or used improperly. Unfortunately, pastors of the television culture tend to view the Internet and e-learning environments as mere extensions of television media. They want to stream their monologue sermons online as if the Internet were just another cable channel. But the key to relational e-learning is relationships. E-learning is not simply a delivery system for information. E-learning is a mechanism for disciples to be instructed in a very personal manner directly by your church's teaching staff.

E-learning occurs in three primary formats: synchronous, asynchronous and hybrid. Synchronous learning occurs when the learning facilitators and students meet online together at a set time and work through lesson content in a group as if they were together in a physical classroom. The chess-master online instruction is a good example of synchronous learning. While various tools such as Skype, WebEx and the like make live group instruction and interaction quite easy to accomplish, synchronous learning contends with the Internet value of individual freedom. The Internet is about freedom—freedom of expression and freedom to learn what we want to learn when we want to learn it. For this reason, synchronous learning comprises at most about 15 percent of all online learning.

Asynchronous learning allows an individual to participate in the learning experience whenever and wherever the student desires. Asynchronous learning is very popular and comprises about 40 percent of all online learning. Critics of asynchronous learning generally point out that little relational interaction takes place during asynchronous learning. This is an unfortunate perception generally validated by poorly implemented asynchronous learning environments. All too often asynchronous learning environments have been constructed and implemented by iron-epoch educators who, in their attempt to be culturally relevant, incorrectly view asynchronous e-learning as a "build it and they will come" or "wind it up and let it go" hands-off learning environment. But it is not uncommon for other online education professionals to experience a greater relational dynamic online than they do within their traditional classrooms.

In 2012 the Pew Internet and American Life Project polled education professionals regarding their current and potentially future use of e-learning. Ed Lyell, a professor at Adams State College and a consultant for using telecommunications to improve school effectiveness through the creation of twenty-first-century learning communities, commented,

> I have taught Internet courses for over a decade now. My interaction with students is often much more involved and significant with the online students than with the classroom students who avoid interaction. Lurkers can get passed in either model unless the professor makes it a point to force students to get involved and expose their ideas to others.[9]

Cyndy Woods-Wilson, an adjunct faculty member at Rio Salado Community College in Tempe, Arizona, and content manager for the LinkedIn group Higher Education Teaching and Learning, expounds on the strategies that educators are now using to facilitate asynchronous education:

> There is a need for speed, and fortunately we've got it. Universities are quickly adapting content delivery modes from all face-to-face to using free online modalities like Facebook groups, Twitter hashtags and Google Plus circles. Not only does it allow higher education to change from costly on-site installations of software (and subsequent upgrades), it allows students to use familiar tools to explore the unfamiliar. Individualized learner outcomes exist naturally within the cloud-computing atmosphere, as students choose their level of commitment and involvement in the group. Should they need to re-visit comments, webinars, etc., they are able to do so at their own time. Students will quickly self-select times they learn best, rather than artificial "class-times" set by a rigid scheduling need. And really, isn't that what education is all about?[10]

Church leaders are generally so accustomed to large group monologue instruction that they easily overlook the great benefit of personalized discipleship strategies. The great benefit of relational disciple making as compared with programmed disciple making is that within the relational context people are able to support one another, with the help of their pastor and peers, as each disciple struggles to live the sanctifying life that is possible only when lived by the Spirit (see Rom. 8:13–14; 1 Cor. 3:1; Gal. 5:16 among others).

9

Community in the Internet-Influenced Church

Aloneness can lead to loneliness. God's preventative for loneliness is intimacy—meaningful, open, sharing relationships with one another. In Christ we have the capacity for the fulfilling sense of belonging which comes from intimate fellowship with God and with other believers.

Neil T. Anderson

The third mission directive of the church is that we are called to establish Christ-centered relational community that nurtures and supports our members. Hebrews 10:25 charges Christ's church not to be "giving up meeting together, as some are in the habit of doing, but encouraging one another—*and all the more as you see the Day approaching*" (and "the Day approaching" is even nearer for those of the Internet-influenced church than it was for generations of the past).

I find the phrase "meeting together" very intriguing. In early church culture meeting together would imply gathering together in local synagogues and/or in the homes of various Christ followers. Today the synagogue is no longer culturally in vogue and has been generally replaced by the big-box buildings that we now call worship centers. Certainly we may still meet together in homes. But can we also meet together in ways that the biblical writers never would have imagined? The answer is yes.

The Web 2.0+ and 3.0 Internet of our day is all about relationships. Yet the iron-epoch culture does not generally interpret the Internet as relational. For the iron-epoch culture, relationships can only exist when people meet in the same room and can see and touch each other. While relationships certainly are forged according to the iron-feet paradigm, they are formed in other ways as well.

The builder generation, also dubbed the greatest generation, understood that sound relationships could be forged and maintained through pen pals. In fact, it was not uncommon for men and women of that generation to have courted via the written word. The builder generation knew that the written word often conveyed feelings and thoughts more precisely and passionately than verbal words could. As an example, look at the revealing words of President Harry S. Truman, who made it his habit to write his heart to Bess, his wife:

> Tomorrow I'll be forty-nine and for all the good I've done the forty might as well be left off. Take it all together

though the experience has been worthwhile; I'd like to do it again. I've been in a railroad, bank, farm, war, politics, love (only once and it still sticks), been busted and still am and yet I have stayed an idealist. I still believe that my sweetheart is the ideal woman and that my daughter is her duplicate. I think that for all the horrors of war it still makes a man if he's one to start with. Politics should make a thief, a rogue, and a pessimist of anyone, but I don't believe I'm any of them and if I can get the Kansas City courthouse done without scandal no other judge will have done as much, and then maybe I can retire as collector and you and the young lady can take some European and South American tours when they'll do you most good; or maybe go to live in Washington and see all the greats and near greats in action. We'll see. I'm counting the days till I see you.

Lots of love to you both, Harry[1]

The Internet-influenced church also understands the communication value of the written word. Through e-mail, instant messaging, chat rooms, discussion forums, blog communities and text messaging, the clay-epoch culture is in constant relational connection with friends and family. In the year 2000, only five years after the release of Windows 95, which made the Internet pervasive, many people argued that the Internet would destroy authentic relationships. As a result, the Pew Internet and American Life Project conducted a survey of Internet users. Their findings help us understand why relational dynamics via the Internet have only increased.

The survey found that the Internet has the opposite of an isolating effect on most users. They report that email has helped them improve their key social relations and expand their social networks. In general, Internet users have more robust social lives than non-users.[2]

Yet the boomer generation remained unconvinced. So on January 25, 2006, the Pew Internet and American Life Project once again completed an extensive study on Internet relationships in an attempt to finally put to rest the debate over whether authentic relationships could possibly be made online. I quote the survey summary below to emphasize this very important point:

> What is [the Internet] doing to the relationships and social capital that Americans have with friends, relatives, neighbors, and workmates? . . . People routinely integrate it into the ways in which they communicate with each other, moving between phone, computer, and in-person encounters. Our evidence calls into question fears that social relationships—and community—are fading away in America. Instead of disappearing, people's communities are transforming: The traditional human orientation to neighborhood- and village-based groups is moving towards communities that are oriented around geographically dispersed social networks. People communicate and maneuver in these networks rather than being bound up in one solitary community. Yet people's networks continue to have substantial numbers of relatives and neighbors—the traditional bases of community—as well as friends and workmates. . . . With the help of the internet, people are able to maintain active contact with

sizable social networks, even though many of the people in those networks do not live nearby. Moreover, there is media multiplexity: The more that people see each other in person and talk on the phone, the more they use the internet. The connectedness that the internet and other media foster within social networks has real payoffs.[3]

When I speak on this issue at ministry and leadership conferences, I commonly receive objections from pastors of the iron-epoch culture. They are quick to claim the benefits of nonverbal visual communication: being able to see how people sit, to make eye contact, to use hand gestures. They claim that our nonverbal actions communicate more than we possibly could with words alone.

Said one young woman, "If people really matter to us, why would we let a week or two go by without talking with them? I am in constant connection with my friends."

I concede that there is great value in nonverbal visual communication. And, by the way, the later versions of the Internet fully support multiplex video community . However, even keeping the Internet's video capacity in mind, the fallacy in the assertion that the Internet destroys genuine relationships is that all communication has to be visual in order for a relationship to be authentic.

Do those of the iron-epoch culture use telephones? Of course they do. Do telephones aid the relationship process?

Of course they do. It is a mistake to believe that those in the clay-epoch culture do not value face-to-face relationships. Authentic relationships are absolutely vital to the clay-epoch culture. In fact, they are so vital that they use various Internet communication mediums to maintain their relational connections 24/7/365. People of the clay-epoch culture appeal to a relational principle called constant connection. As one young woman expressed to me, "If people really matter to us, why would we let a week or two go by without talking with them? I am in constant connection with my friends."[4]

In the spring of 2006, I spoke at a conference in Tennessee. During the conference I received a phone call from my hometown pastor asking if I could pick up his daughter from college on my return trip so that she could spend the weekend with her family. I had to drive by the college anyway, so I agreed. Over the nine hours of our trip, this twenty-year-old college student constantly sent and received text messages. We talked together about the dynamics of the Internet culture, and she affirmed that she could not imagine life without being able to connect with her friends whenever and wherever she wished.

It is important that we contrast this college student's constant-connection mind-set with the mind-set of many iron-epoch pastors. Most pastors today would likely perceive the endless barrage of text messages, phone calls and Facebook posts as an intrusion into their private life. In fact, when I build websites for iron-epoch pastors, it is common that the pastor refuses to receive e-mail or phone communications via the church website. E-mail communications from the church website, if they are permitted at all, generally go to a church secretary. The typical iron-epoch pastor simply does not want to be bothered with communications that he or she has not initiated.

A January 2004 Barna update summary asserted that 55 percent of the churches they studied would not even answer the church phone![5] While the clay-epoch culture values being always connected, the iron-epoch culture, in contrast, often seeks to disconnect and isolate themselves from the outside world. The boomer's attitude is literally "out of sight, out of mind"—and we turn the television off with a flick of our remote control.

Some time ago I was participating in an online discussion regarding the relational dynamics of the Internet generation. One of the discussion participants explained why she so deeply valued online relationships:

> I think a very cool thing about the world of cyber-relations is that it takes the emphasis off appearance. Yahweh said to Samuel, "Man looks at the outward appearance, but God looks at the heart." I like the fact that I don't see many of your outward appearances, rather *I gain better access to your hearts* via the written word. I am set free from the power of my visual perception.

I highlighted the words "I gain better access to your hearts" because it is important that we explore this assertion. Within the Internet culture there is another principle I glossed over previously that I call "intimacy at a distance."

I have used this phrase since 2002 to describe a very unique and common Internet behavior, namely, that when people are online, they very quickly become vulnerable. It is common for people participating in online discussions to share their struggles, hopes and fears openly and honestly. In fact, the depth of discussion that can often be reached in thirty or forty minutes online may take many months to achieve using the traditional small-group paradigm advocated by churches within the iron-epoch culture.

In 2003, following the launch of my ministry E-Church Essentials, I spoke to a gathering of pastors and staff at an emergent ministry luncheon regarding the principle of intimacy at a distance. When I made the assertion that online discussions can help pastors penetrate the protective outward facades that we all display and discover people's felt-need issues much more quickly than is possible using traditional shepherding practices, one church staffer raised her hand and asked if she could comment on this point.

She stood up and began to explain how she had heard about the principle of intimacy at a distance and so decided to go online and explore this principle for herself. She soon found herself in an online discussion with another young woman who was deeply hurting. Within twenty minutes this young woman was literally "dumping" her pain onto the chat room screen so quickly that this megachurch staffer began to panic and had to exit the chat room—she had never before experienced people becoming so vulnerable so quickly. This staffer confessed to the audience that she had been personally and professionally unprepared for the relational realities of intimacy at a distance.

Intimacy at a distance provides the church with an incredible platform for relational community and discipleship. If the goal of any healthy church is to make disciples of Jesus Christ, then the process must begin by establishing authentic relationships that enable both the disciple and the rabbi-teacher to become vulnerable and honest about their personal and spiritual lives. Web-based discipleship strategies open the door for ministry professionals and laity to develop these open and honest relationships with others very quickly. The result can be an intense and vulnerable relationship that would otherwise take many months or possibly years to develop using traditional ministry methods.

As we have learned, relationships are a core value of the Internet-influenced church. How can two different cultures—the clay-epoch culture and the iron-epoch culture—share a core value and yet misunderstand each other so dramatically? It is difficult to comprehend. However, the misunderstanding is quite real. The established iron-epoch church culture typically accuses the people of the clay-epoch culture of not being capable of developing real or authentic relationships, while the clay-epoch culture accuses the people of the iron-epoch culture of showmanship and relational hypocrisy.

For the clay-epoch culture, there is nothing more relationally shallow than the interactions that occur only once a week at most church services and in church lobbies before and after the service. This "fellowship time," so labeled by iron-epoch churches, is for many people of the clay-epoch culture, who value deep and sincere relationships, a misnomer at best and at its worse a weekly exercise at church-sanctioned lying. Everybody wears a smile, telling one another that they are fine, while their discussion remains socially safe. One postmodern ministry contracted E-Church Essentials to develop marketing strategies for them related to surveyed issues that they had found kept people in their community from attending church. Social insincerity in the church lobby was one of the leading issues identified in their surveys. The resulting marketing campaign concept is depicted in the illustration below:

While the graphic may seem unfair to people accustomed to the church lobby experience, the point is that when a cultural divide exists, what is valued by one culture can become a stumbling block for another.

A number of years ago I was speaking with a leader from an internationally known megachurch ministry that had been founded upon television-culture principles. We were discussing some technological innovations that I believed could help address people-related issues that the church was experiencing. The staffer bluntly told me, "We will never allow computers in our church. Computers are not relational."

Over the years I have heard this sentiment passionately extolled by many church pastors who serve an iron-epoch, television-influenced church. With such strong negative opinions regarding the integration of computer and Internet technology into ministry, these leaders literally dismiss the cultural realities and values of scores of millions of people who comprise the clay-epoch culture. Computers are essential to this culture. From communication, banking, job search, education and relationships, computers are integrated into their cultural fabric.

To help make the point, let's contrast various aspects of daily living and how the two distinct generations often deal differently with life's demands.

Life Task	Iron-Epoch Culture	Clay-Epoch Culture
Banking	Uses checkbook, cash, typically uses manual accounting.	Uses electronic banking, auto deposits, auto-bill pay, finance software, does not typically write paper checks.
Information Searching	Makes use of traditional dictionaries, encyclopedias and occasionally search engines.	Uses search engines constantly as well as various wiki platforms such as Wikipedia. May not even own a paper dictionary or encyclopedia.
Dating	Meets people locally and dates locally.	Uses online-dating services and social-networking services to meet people with complementary profiles.
Entertainment	Watches television at home and movies at a traditional theater.	Prefers Internet-based activities over television; prefers online videos and home theater over traditional theater.
Relationships	Local relationships are based upon shared interests, clubs and church affiliations.	Local and global relationships are based upon shared interests and life experiences and maintained via the Internet.
Education	Educational culture takes place within a classroom environment hosted in a brick-and-mortar facility.	Educational culture is either enhanced through online learning environments or is 100 percent online.

Without taking time to expand upon each category listed in this table, I want to illustrate how the cultural shift in banking practices challenges one aspect of the iron-epoch ture's sense of a worship community.

People of the Internet-influenced church do not typically write paper checks or carry cash. They are accustomed to handling almost all transactions electronically. As a result, when the offering plate goes by each Sunday, they likely do not put anything in the plate. This does not mean, however, that they are unwilling to tithe, as so often they are accused of being. They simply tithe in a different way.

Clay-epoch churches—and a growing number of iron-epoch churches—have learned the value of configuring an electronic donation subscription on their website. Depending upon the specific church culture and how well it promotes the online donation feature, these churches generally receive 15 to 30 percent of their support—their most stable income—via this e-commerce medium. In the years to come, this percentage will only increase. Within a few decades it is conceivable that the offering plate will be a thing of the past. In its place will be a gift box in the back of the auditorium for those few remaining traditionalists who still prefer to give using cash or paper checks, while the majority of giving within the local church will take place electronically. Mars Hill of Grandville, Michigan, is an excellent example of this paradigm shift in action. Mars Hill does not pass an offering plate but makes use of gift boxes near the exits of the auditorium. However, it also has a high-quality online "support this ministry" e-commerce interface on their website.

My family shares the banking values of the clay-epoch culture, and typically we do not place our offering in the offering plate on Sunday. Rather, we have configured our automated bill-pay system to electronically deposit our tithe to the church every two weeks. Yet I must confess that when the plate goes by each Sunday, I feel a false twinge of guilt because the people around me do not observe my family supporting the church. This is unfortunate, because when people of the clay-epoch culture configure electronic funds transfers, they are honoring the principle of first fruits taught in Scripture (see Deut. 26:1–15; Rom. 8:23–25). Consistent firstfruits e-tithing demonstrates that giving back to the Lord is a priority in one's personal budget.

When iron-epoch leaders insist that the offering plate is the only legitimate means of giving tithes and offerings, they communicate to the clay-epoch culture how out of touch they are with its cultural norms. The unintentional message is, "My culture is spiritual; your culture is not."

Wise leadership acknowledges that a culture shift indeed exists and publically assures its membership that tithing can occur in many different ways as appropriate to the individual's culture. It should not be important how we tithe. Rather, it is important that all Christ followers acknowledge the lordship of Jesus Christ and give Him the firstfruits of their finances, time and talents.

A Christ-centered community extends far beyond the concept of tithing within a local congregation. From Facebook friends, Yahoo groups and Google circles to interactive blogs, discussion forums and relational e-learning communities, the concept of community now extends beyond the local into the global and so has now been rightly defined as "glocal."

10

Equipping in the Internet-Influenced Church

Our inventions are wont to be pretty toys, which distract our attention from serious things. They are but improved means to an unimproved end, an end which it was already but too easy to arrive at.

Henry David Thoreau, *Walden*

I have no desire to offend Sue Mallory, for she at least has tried to persuade the local church to equip people for ministry service, but I have often heard it said that the title of her book *The Equipping Church* is an oxymoron. Indeed, in many churches today little equipping, which is our fourth mission directive, takes place. Ephesians 4:11–12 relates the church's equipping obligation clearly, particularly to those whom the Holy Spirit has called to be apostles, prophets, evangelists, pastors and teachers, that they should "equip his people for works of service." Why is it then that so little equipping takes place?

The Internet does not have a better handle on the ministry of equipping than its predecessor the television. Henry David Thoreau was right: our inventions—in this case the Internet—are nothing more than "pretty toys" that could easily distract the Internet-influenced church from implementing an intentional equipping ministry rather than inform it. Whether the cultural medium is television or the Internet, Christ challenges His church to take the command to equip people for ministry seriously. So why doesn't Christ's church do a better job at equipping? I submit that one major reason is that sincere Christian leaders are often confused about what equipping people for ministry service looks like.

On a practical level pastors often confuse making disciples (see Matt. 28:19) and equipping disciples (see Eph. 4:11–12). To a certain extent this confusion is understandable, since the process of becoming and growing as a disciple of Christ and the process of being equipped as a disciple of Christ are both essential for developing mature Christ followers. However, it is important to understand the differences between these two ministry functions. In order for us to parse those differences, it may be helpful for us to have descriptive definitions for each mission priority. I define these two ministry priorities as follows:

> *Making Disciples:* The intentional investment of a person or organization into the life of another, helping mature an individual's love for Christ and his or her faith in Christ

that is founded upon a growing knowledge of God's will according to the Scriptures and the ongoing submission of self to the guiding and sanctifying power of the Holy Spirit.

Mobilizing Disciples: A partnership between a spiritual mentor and a disciple created to help the disciple discern God's purpose (or call) for his or her life based upon an assessment of his or her unique design, the nurturing and affirmation of his or her corresponding spiritual gifts and the training and testing of the disciple in real-life ministry opportunities before unleashing the disciple to serve.

As I reflect upon these two definitions, I suspect that your reaction may be the same as mine: *These definitions do not describe the journey of my personal spiritual formation nor of my preparation for ministry service.* Certainly I attended Sunday school and youth group as a child. And later in life I attended college and seminary. Yet through all those diverse activities, not one experience came close to fulfilling the definitions provided. Why? The interpersonal dynamic was always missing. In most every church-related event I attended, I was taught biblical information but was never mentored to help me apply the information to my life. It felt to me as if living the Christian life was something I had to figure out for myself.

To make matters worse, my personality did not fit the "preferred" pastoral ministry profile. I was too entrepreneurial, too creative, too task-focused, too driven. Rather than help match me to an appropriate area of ministry service, my denomination rejected me. This was a very painful experience in my life. I felt as if I was being told that the person God had made me to be and the gifts He had given me to serve Him were somehow unacceptable. But the Lord was faithful and guided me into entrepreneurial ministry ventures such as church revitalization, church planting, church consulting and ministry software design.

I have mentioned some of my own struggles with being equipped and mobilized into ministry simply to illustrate what I believe is an extreme example. I realize that there are some churches that may be doing an outstanding job in equipping and mobilizing people into ministry service. However, such equipping churches are the exception and not the norm.

In 2002 I designed a series of assessments intended to aid churches in their efforts to mobilize people into ministry service. These assessments first appeared as a module within our E-Church Network platform and later, in 2006, as a stand-alone program called AssessME.org. I have had the opportunity to observe thousands of churches since 2002. What I have noticed in most churches is that they will assess people for ministry fit and then plug people into appropriate ministry roles while completely sidestepping the equipping-for-ministry phase.

Sadly, the art of equipping people for ministry service was largely lost during the television-influenced church era. In many cases people today are placed into ministry roles that support the church's programming with little or no equipping whatsoever. Church leaders seldom consider the individual's personal ministry calling or seek to support that calling, especially if that call causes the individual to serve Christ outside the programming structures of the local church. Some may find it unfair to say so, but it often seems that church leaders' actions portray the attitude that they value their church programming more than the individuals who support that programming. And the many people who are not able to support the church's programming generally receive no equipping-for-ministry support at all.

The Internet-influenced church will have to restore the mission of equipping people for ministry as the second-most important directive Christ has given His church and implement it in such a way that it is relevant to the present and emerging culture.

So what impact will this well-established dysfunction have upon the Internet-influenced church? The Internet-influenced church will have to restore the mission of equipping people for ministry as the second-most important directive Christ has given His church and implement it in such a way that it is relevant to the present and emerging culture. Whatever form this may ultimately take, the methodology should be based upon the Holy Spirit's initial intent—that apostles, prophets, evangelists, pastors and teachers will all work together to equip people for the works of service. These five-fold ministry functions describe the kinds of service roles necessary to make a local church healthy, vibrant and reproducible. Look at their definitions below:

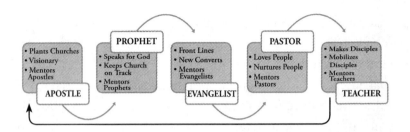

- *Apostles.* Apostles are entrepreneurial ministry leaders responsible for new ministry development (church planting, new church programs, new systems, etc.). These church leaders should be responsible for equipping younger individuals with a similar ministry calling.

- *Prophets.* The traditional biblical role for a prophet is to publicly declare God's will and purpose and to expose individual and community sin, particularly when God's people decide to do what is "right in their own eyes" (Judg. 21:25, NLT). Prophets should equip younger individuals who possess a similar ministry calling.

- *Evangelists.* Evangelists are front-line ministry leaders who are passionate about leading others to Christ. These individuals often hang out at shopping malls and bars in an effort to meet non-Christians, build a trusting relationship with them and then share the gospel message with them. Evangelists should equip younger individuals who possess a similar ministry calling.

- *Pastors.* Pastors are responsible to care for the physical, emotional and spiritual needs of people within the church. Pastors are highly relational people. Pastors should equip younger individuals who possess a similar ministry calling.

- *Teachers.* Teachers are individuals who are passionate about communicating the Word of God to people within the church. These individuals understand that making disciples occurs largely through teaching people to obey all that Christ has commanded. Teaching occurs not only at the corporate level but also in small groups and in one-on-one mentorships. Teachers should equip younger individuals who possess a similar ministry calling.

If you are familiar with the AssessME.org program, then its leadership style assessment is not entirely new to you. However, for those who do not understand this tool, please let me explain the parallels that exist between this assessment and the five-fold leadership model just outlined.

The leadership style assessment plots an individual on a continuum from entrepreneurial and task driven on the left side to highly social and task avoidant on the right side. That continuum then divides into three broad segments: builders, managers and nurturers. Each segment is then subdivided into two leadership style descriptions. The leadership style assessment, although a psychometric tool, compares very closely to the five-fold ministry.

The leadership style continuum may look like this:

The Five-Fold Leadership Style Continuum

Entrepreneurial and Task Driven . . . . Highly Social and Task Avoidant

The Holy Spirit gave the church a leadership model that was designed to care for the needs of the local church, equip people for ministry and mobilize people into Kingdom service. Unfortunately, many churches ignore this model all together or translate these categories into church "offices," which then significantly restricts these functions to the five "authorized" types of leaders. It is better to view the five categories as a systemic structure intended to mobilize entire congregations into service.

The Internet-influenced church will need to assimilate an appropriate version of this equipping and mobilizing model into their concept of being the church, and I am confident that it will, for Ephesians 4:13 asserts that these five equipping functions will occur "until we all reach unity in the faith and in the knowledge of the Son of God and become mature, attaining to the whole measure of the fullness of Christ." The little word "until" tells us that the Holy Spirit will ensure that these equipping functions will continue in some form throughout the Christian era, for we have not yet all reached "unity in the faith" nor "unity . . . in the knowledge of the Son of God," nor have we all become "mature, attaining to the whole measure of the fullness of Christ." The church may stray from time to time from what the Holy Spirit has ordained, but the Holy Spirit will ensure that at all times God's will shall be done "on earth as it is in heaven" (Matt. 6:10).

11

Loving One Another in the Internet-Influenced Church

Love is not a feeling. Love is an action, an activity. . . .
Genuine love implies commitment and the exercise of wis-
dom . . . love as the will to extend oneself for the purpose
of nurturing one's own or another's spiritual growth. . . .
True love is an act of will that often transcends ephemeral
feelings of love or cathexis, it is correct to say,
"Love is as love does."

Scott Peck, *The Road Less Traveled*

S cott Peck wrote those words prior to his book's publi-
cation in 1996. This is the very point in time at which
Microsoft enabled the Internet to become public to
the average person via Windows 95.

The two opposing cultures—the television-influenced
church and the Internet-influenced church—implement

Peck's definition of love differently. From the jaded perspective of the television-influenced church, they often look at the hundreds of Facebook "friends" their teenagers may have and think, *How far we have fallen.* For Facebook friends are seldom friends indeed, a fact that the Internet-influenced church would affirm.

Romans 13:8 commands Christ followers to "let no debt remain outstanding, except the continuing debt to love one another, for whoever loves others has fulfilled the law." The Internet-influenced church will fulfill this debt of love, our fifth and final mission directive, and will love one another in word (online and in person) and deed (through glocal mission outreach). But it will love differently than did the television-influenced church. In the previous era most all mission funds and activities were funneled through the local church. However, the Internet-influenced church will love collaboratively through an immense communication network and various relational mediums that are quite foreign to the television-influenced church. Even Pope Francis recognized this emerging reality in his 2013 *Evangelii Gaudium*:

> Today, when the networks and means of human communication have made unprecedented advances, we sense the challenge of finding and sharing a "mystique" of living together, of mingling and encounter, of embracing and supporting one another, of stepping into this flood tide which, while chaotic, can become a genuine experience of fraternity, a caravan of solidarity, a sacred pilgrimage. Greater possibilities for communication thus turn into

greater possibilities for encounter and solidarity for everyone. If we were able to take this route, it would be so good, so soothing, so liberating and hope-filled! To go out of ourselves and to join others is healthy for us. To be self-enclosed is to taste the bitter poison of immanence, and humanity will be worse for every selfish choice we make.[1]

The walls that separated societies during the television-influenced church era are now crumbling, and the potential for extending Christ's love into all the world has never been more possible.

The walls that separated societies during the television-influenced church era are now crumbling, and the potential for extending Christ's love into all the world has never been more possible. One current example of this reality is Global Media Outreach. This organization has provided a worthwhile mission tool that has served Christ's church for some time. Its system empowers pastors and parishioners to personally share Christ with people from almost every country in the world from the comfort of their own living rooms or offices. It also enables people to be personally discipled by another Christ follower entirely online. Global Media Outreach's website offers a remarkable statistic:

> 10 years ago, GMO asked, "What if we put the gospel online? Would people care?" Since then, more than 100 million people have not only cared—they've believed. 100

million out of 7 billion just scratches the surface. Will you help reach the rest? The world is searching online.[2]

Let's consider this statistic for the moment. If we assume that Global Media Outreach is honest with their statistics, then approximately ten million people have accepted Jesus Christ as their Lord and Savior each year since it started via the Internet. In comparison, the Hartford Institute for Religion Research offers the following statistics regarding physical churches in North America :[3]

Attendance	# of churches	Weekly worshipers	Percent
7-99	177,000	9 million	59%
100-499	105,000	25 million	35%
500-999	12,000	9 million	4%
1,000-1,999	6,000	8 million	2%
2,000-9,999	1,170	4 million	.4%
10,000-plus	40	.7 million	.01%
TOTALS	approx. 300,000	approx. 56 million	100%

So in order to keep up with just one online mission portal, the average American church must make 33.33 new converts to Christ each year. There may be some churches that can meet or exceed this number easily. However, I have seen year-end reports from various denominations that show an average of less than five adult conversions per church per year. Just imagine the disparity that will exist between the brick-and-mortar church and the Internet-influenced church once online-enhanced missions become commonplace.

The television-influenced church has been very slow to make the transition to online ministry. It will undoubtedly be up to the millennials, the first true Internet generation, to lead the way in this shift.

The millennial trend toward social action as a means of expressing love for the planet, its ecology and its people is already apparent, and it does not look to decline in popularity any time soon. The Internet-influenced church is quite globally aware. Furthermore, it has the technical, and often the financial, means to make a difference. However, there are forces at work that, if unchecked by Christ's church, may actually impede mission impact by the Internet-influenced culture.

Postmodern business takes advantage of this emerging culture's desire to make a difference by incorporating what is known as cause marketing into product marketing campaigns. For example, the Chicago Better Business Bureau reports on "Pink Washing":

> "Pinkwashing or Pinkwashers are businesses that purposely misuse pink ribbon marketing to promote products and/or services that provide little or no benefit to breast cancer causes," says Steve J. Bernas, president and CEO of the Better Business Bureau serving Chicago and Northern Illinois. "That's why it is extremely important for donors to—think before they pink—or they could find that the dollars they chose to spend did nothing more than fill the

coffers of or line the pockets of some less than scrupulous businesses or individuals."[4]

The damage from such practices to this culture's missional philanthropy is even more severe than the inevitable jadedness that accompanies bait-and-switch marketing. Cause marketing has been shown to actually decrease overall giving to mission causes as well as decrease personal participation in support of mission causes.

Aradhna Krishna is a researcher for the University of Michigan. In 2011 she summarized her findings in an article published by the *Toronto Star*:

> I would like to point you to work on "moral licensing." Moral licensing says that if people have done a good deed, then they are less likely to do a second good deed. A slew of research studies by social psychologists have shown evidence for moral licensing. For instance, if people make a decision to hire a woman, they are less likely to do so in a second unrelated hiring job, even if she is the best candidate in the set; if they vote for a black president—yes, think Barack Obama—then they are more likely to be openly racist later; and if they buy green products, then they feel less bad about driving a gas-guzzler. So it is no surprise that direct donations decrease after a charity has been supported through cause marketing.[5]

The church that navigates the challenges of evolving from a television-influenced church to an Internet-influenced church can itself become caught up in cause marketing. Promoting good causes in and of themselves will likely result in an overall decrease in tithing and personal ministry involvement by church members. Cause marketing can easily become a cheap substitute for promoting Jesus Christ and can replace His love as our primary motivation for mission and for offering His salvation to all who will accept—which is the ultimate goal of our ministry and mission efforts.

Scott Peck was right—love is an action, not merely a feeling. However, love is more than mere action, love is a person: Jesus Christ. It must be His love that compels the Internet-influenced church to extend that love to others. Selfish, altruistic feelings of contributing a few cause marketing dollars to help make the world a better place is a poor substitute for the love of Jesus Christ.

Conclusion

Final Thoughts

When I stand before God at the end of my life, I would hope that I would not have a single bit of talent left, and could say, "I used everything you gave me."

Erma Bombeck

---

cclesiastes 1:9 tells us that "there is nothing new under the sun." While some may argue that Solomon was in error, since the Internet is something new, what the Internet enables humanity to accomplish is as old as humanity is itself. Humanity has always sought a means for us to *relate* to one another and to our Creator; to *communicate* for purposes of emotional, intellectual and spiritual support; to *collaborate* together over tasks that cannot be accomplished alone and to *facilitate* important learning and application that helps give life meaning and purpose. These are the interpersonal interactions that we might summarize in the term "media."

As such, we err when we confuse the medium for the media. Though the original Latin medias may not make such distinctions, today we must differentiate the means (medium) from the message (media). For mediums do indeed transform over time: from oral tradition to written word, from telegraph to radio, from television to Internet to who knows what in the future. Mediums change. But media is the emotional, intellectual and practical interaction that never changes.

Medium does impose itself into our media message. As mediums change over time, the nature of communication, and interpersonal relationships by extension, also change. For example, in the era of the written word, letters could be as long as needed to convey the necessary message. However, when the telegraph was invented, it increased the speed of communication while simultaneously reducing media's content to succinct text messages. Just so, media via television must communicate differently than media via Internet. As such, the medium itself greatly influences the culture in which it is used, transforming how humanity relates, communicates, collaborates and facilitates. Two mediums cannot easily coexist in culture, for mediums have the potential of defining what culture shall be. One medium must give way to another that proves more efficient and effective. So while two mediums may hold influence upon differing segments of society, those societal groups will likely be in tension with one another. Differing mediums naturally impose a distinct perspective and paradigm for how individuals understand and interact with the world around them.

The Internet-influenced church seeks to regain what they believe has been lost: the intimacy of a real faith walk with the Spirit of Christ and with one another in a constantly connected community. The Internet-influenced church longs to move beyond forms, traditions and rituals to discover what it really means to live by the Spirit and to allow that same Spirit to help them make a sincere kingdom impact upon a global community that is broken and suffering in sin.

Those of the Internet-influenced church are not image conscious. In every aspect of their life, they seek authenticity and simplicity. They feel that something is broken in today's presentational expression of Christianity, and so the Internet-influenced church attempts to correct the errors they perceive. There is no new ministry model to follow. There is no master plan for church growth for Internet-influenced churches. This new clay-era culture is indigenous to the entire planet. Their flat social structure follows the organizational pattern of the Internet rather than the hierarchy of corporate America, so they prefer grassroots social structures that are only one layer deep.

Ministry in this new era will best occur when church leaders immerse themselves in that single layer and join the community at large as a humble peer. That peer community may feel scary and unfamiliar, but such has been the uncomfortable yet exhilarating feelings experienced by missionaries of past centuries as they entered new worlds in which people had never before known Jesus Christ as Savior and Lord.

So, put simply, what principles ought a pastoral leader to consider when constructing an Internet-influenced church? Here are my top ten suggestions:

1. Make every opportunity for "coming together" (see 1 Cor. 14:26) an *interactive* dialogue; minimize or eliminate monologue communication.

2. Create a culture in which people are free and are expected to *contribute* to the worship community based upon giftedness and spiritual-formation experiences. Consider using daily e-mail or RSS communications to help prepare people to offer insights and application stories that will encourage the body. (Note: A contributive culture is only healthy when church elders gently correct in public any statement or behavior that they believe is inconsistent with God's Word and sound doctrine).

3. Pastoral leaders should serve as *learning facilitators*, helping the worship community to test and apply biblical truth so that each individual may validate God's truth through personal experience. Incorporate e-learning disciple-making solutions that serve not only people within your immediate community but also people from around the world.

4. Take a sincere interest in each person's spiritual development, helping to define for each person an appropriate and unique path for their *spiritual formation*, caring to track each person's development over

time and regularly reviewing and modifying each individual's spiritual-formation plan.

5. Minimize *technology* used for presentational purposes such as stage lighting and screen-projected live video. Rather, use technology to facilitate *relational*, *educational* and *mobilizing* ministry purposes.

6. Develop a creative culture in which people are free to *collaborate* with each other the strategies and methods that best expand Christ's kingdom in their present culture. Through the collaborative process be willing to attempt ministry in ways that have never before been tried.

7. Simplify, simplify, simplify so that when you come together, your worship gathering is humble and sincere, not pretentious or showy, enabling people to feel comfortable and at ease—to be *authentic*. Similarly, ministry leaders must clearly model for others a Christian life that is vulnerable, honest and real.

8. Help young adults make a significant and *positive impact* upon their culture "glocally." Promote local, regional and international ministry opportunities. AssessME.org is an excellent tool to help individuals better understand God's design and call upon their lives.

9. Develop 24/7 evangelistic and pastoral care *live-help services* for any and all people who are in spiritual and emotional need. I have personally used live support

solutions from www.providesupport.com and found
their systems to be very easy to implement and quite
cost effective.

10. Provide opportunities for *personal application* or response as a normative part of all worship gatherings.
Contemplative response is okay, but interactive response stations are even better.

When I first started to write this book, I was tempted to
incorporate recommended software solutions into the various chapters. I ultimately resisted this temptation, because
software solutions come and go as the Internet evolves.
However, the cultural values of the Internet-influenced society will likely last for many years to come. I have no idea
whether the clay-epoch will last one more day or a thousand years. What I do know and can relate with confidence
is that the clay epoch—today's digital age—represents a
global epoch that has forever transformed how society
functions, conducts business, educates, builds and main-
tains relationships—and does church.

We stand on the precipice of a new world order. We can
either go back to Egypt, where we have become comfortable in our presentational ministry dysfunction, or we can
choose to participate in the ongoing reformation. I hope
and trust that our Lord will give each of us the faith and
vision we require to help expand Christ's kingdom as vital
members of the Internet-influenced church.

Notes

PREFACE

1. Scot McKnight, "Five Streams of the Emerging Church: Key Elements of the Most Controversial and Misunderstood Movement in the Church Today," *Christianity Today*, January 2007.

INTRODUCTION

1. Eras of Elegance, "The Renaissance Era (1450–1600)," http://www.erasofelegance.com/history/renaissancescience.html.

2. Gleason L. Archer Jr., trans., *Jerome's Commentary on Daniel* (Grand Rapids: Baker, 1958).

3. John Calvin, *Commentary on Daniel*, vol. 1, trans. Thomas Meyers, M.A. (Grand Rapids: Christian Classics Ethereal Library, 1852).

4. George Booker, "Daniel," *The Agora Bible Commentary*, http://www.christadelphianbooks.org/agora/comm/27_dan/dan03.html.

5. George Rawlinson, *The History of Herodotus*, vol. 1 (New York: D. Appleton and Co., 1885), 178–200.

6. *Encyclopaedia Iranica*, www.IranicaOnline.org .

7. Roman Bronze Recycling Trade, American University TED case study, vol. 1, no. 1, case no. 224, September 1992., www1.american.edu/TED/bronze.htm

8. "Do as the Romans Did (with Statues)—Recycle!" *Palimpsest This!* December 2, 2009, https://ipalimpsest.wordpress.com/2009/12/02/bronzetrade/.

9. David Noy, "'A Sight Unfit to See': Jewish Reactions to the Roman Imperial Cult," *Classics Ireland*, vol. 8, 2001, http://www.classicsireland.com/2001/noy.html.

10. Joseph A. Montagna, "The Industrial Revolution," Yale–New Haven Teachers Institute, http://www.yale.edu/ynhti/curriculum/units/1981/2/81.02.06.x.html.

11. Philipp Laube, "Wafer Fabrication," *Semiconductor Technology from A to Z*, http://www.halbleiter.org/en/waferfabrication/print/.

CHAPTER 1

1. Stewart M. Hoover, Ph.D., Lynn Schofield Clark, Ph.D., and Lee Rainie, "Faith Online: 64% of Wired Americans Have Used the Internet for Spiritual or Religious Purposes," Pew Internet and American Life Project, April 7, 2004, http://www.pewinternet.org/files/old-media/Files/Reports/2004/PIP_Faith_Online_2004.pdf.pdf.

2. Douglas Adams, "How to Stop Worrying and Learn to Love the Internet," *Sunday Times*, August 29, 1999, http://www.douglasadams.com/dna/19990901-00-a.html.

3. Ibid.

4. Marc Prensky, "Digital Natives, Digital Immigrants" in *On the Horizon* (MCB University Press, vol. 9, no. 5, October 2001), http://www.marcprensky.com/writing/Prensky%20-%20Digital%20Natives,%20Digital%20Immigrants%20-%20Part1.pdf.

5. Neil Postman, *Amusing Ourselves to Death: Public Discourse in the Age of Show Business* (New York: Viking Penguin, 1985).

6. Lee Strobel, *Inside the Mind of Unchurched Harry and Mary* (Grand Rapids: Zondervan, 1993).

7. Sheryl Feinstein, *The Praeger Handbook of Learning and the Brain* (Westport, CT: Greenwood, 2006), 439.

8. Morley Safer, *The Millennials Are Coming!* TV Broadcast (New York: CBS News, 2008), http://www.cbsnews.com/videos/the-millennials-are-coming/.

9. "How Long Is a Generation?" *Ancestry.com*. http://www.ancestry. com/cs/Satellite?childpagename=UKLearningCenter%2FLe arning_C%2FPageDefault&pagename=LearningWrapper&c id=1265124426382.

10. Personal interview with Laura Bradford, 2006.

11. Greg Hawkins and Cally Parkinson, *Reveal: Where Are You?* (South Barrington, IL: Willow Creek Association, 2007), 36.

12. Josh Morton, "I'm Tired of Being a Christian," *JoshMorton.com*, November 15, 2012, http://www.joshmorton.com/repost-im-tired-of-being-a-christian/.

13. "A New Generation Expresses Its Skepticism and Frustration with Christianity," Barna Group, September 24, 2007, https://www.barna.org/barna-update/millennials/94-a-new-generation-expresses-its-skepticism-and-frustration-with-christianity#.Uw51aIWLVsU.

14. Open letter on www.SafeFaith.com, 2007 (website now disbanded).

CHAPTER 2

1. Postman, *Amusing Ourselves to Death*, 8.

2. Jon Walker, "Family Life Council Says It's Time to Bring Family Back to Life," *sbc.net*, June 12, 2002, http://www.sbcannual-meeting.net/sbc02/newsroom/newspage.asp?ID=261.

3. Postman, *Amusing Ourselves to Death*, 18.

4. Ibid., 28.

CHAPTER 3

1. "Congregations Say the Internet Helps Their Spiritual and Community Life," *PewResearch Internet Project*, December 20, 2000, http://www.pewinternet.org/2000/12/20/congregations-say-the-internet-helps-their-spiritual-and-community-life/.

2. "The Cyberchurch: A Study by the Barna Institute," The Barna Research Group, Ltd. 2001, 4.

3. Jonathan Strickland, "How Web 3.0 Will Work," *howstuffworks. com*, http://computer.howstuffworks.com/web-304.htm.

4. "HTML5 Introduction," *w3schools.com*, http://www.w3schools. com/html/html5_intro.asp.

5. Tim O'Reilly, "What is Web 2.0: Design Patterns and Business Models for the Next Generation of Software," *O'Reilly*, September 30, 2005, http://oreilly.com/web2/archive/what-is-web-20.html.

6. Mary Madden, "Music, Interrupted," *PewResearch Internet Project*, May 9, 2007 http://www.pewinternet.org/Commentary/2007/May/Music-interrupted.aspx.

CHAPTER 4

1. "The New Rebel Cry: Jesus Is Coming!" *Time* magazine, June 21, 1971.

2. Ed Stetzer, "Understanding the Charismatic Movement," *Christianity Today*, October 18, 2013, http://www. christianitytoday.com/edstetzer/2013/october/charismatic-renewal-movement.html.

3. "A Charismatic Time Was Had by All," *Time* magazine, August 8, 1977.

4. "Is Your Church Leadership Graying?" United Methodist Communications, http://www.umcom.org/site/apps/nlnet/content3.aspx?c=mrLZJ9PFKmG&b=8727411&ct=7728083&notoc=1.

5. "Quitting Church: A Q&A with Julia Duin," *beliefnet*, http://www.beliefnet.com/columnists/textmessages/2009/02/quitting-church-a-qa-with-juli.html#ixzz2qVXrFB5H.

6. Sally Morgenthaler, "Worship as Evangelism," *Rev!* May/June 2007, http://www.baptist.org. au/site/DefaultSite/filesystem/documents/ MorgenthalerSallyWorshipAsEvangelismRevMag%20 %283%29.pdf.

7. Wayne Jacobsen, "Just What Is the Church? An Open Letter to Tim Stafford," *Life Stream*, January 21, 2005, http://lifestream. org/waynes-blog/just-what-church.

8. Brian Zahnd, message given at CMI 37th Annual Convention , Fort Wayne, Indiana. September 23, 2008.

9. Haines, Michael, National Center for Health Statistics in Jonathan V. Last's, "America's Baby Bust," Wall Street Journal, February 12, 2013

10. "Most Twentysomethings Put Christianity on the Shelf Following Spiritually Active Teen Years," Barna Group, September 11, 2006, https://www.barna.org/barna-update/ millennials/147-most-twentysomethings-put-christianity-on- the-shelf-following-spiritually-active-teen-years#.Utf_udiA2zc.

11. Hoover, Schofield Clark and Rainie, "Faith Online."

12. "Microsoft Accessibility," Microsoft Corporation, http://www. microsoft.com/enable/microsoft/mission.aspx.

CHAPTER 5

1. Gospel Coalition, http://thegospelcoalition.org/about/who.

2. JusticeJones, "I Am My Own God," *Experience Project*, July 7, 2013. http://www.experienceproject.com/stories/Am-My- Own-God/3300299.

CHAPTER 6

1. Definition of *beneficium, Free Dictionary*, http://encyclopedia2. thefreedictionary.com/Beneficium.

2. Fr. Andreas Hoeck, S.S.D., "Holy Communion: Sharing in the Threefold Munus of the Divine Gladiator," *Homiletic & Pastoral Review*, June 7, 2013, http://www.hprweb.com/2013/06/holy-communion-sharing-in-the-threefold-munus-of-the-divine-gladiator/.

3. Definition of *officium*, *Encyclo Online Encyclopedia*, http://www.encyclo.co.uk/define/officium.

4. Christopher Dorn, "The Emergent Church and Worship," *Reformed Review*, vol. 61, no. 3, fall 2008: 136.

5. Rad Zdero, Grassroots Christianity Brochure, http://www.scribd.com/doc/79043324/Grassroots-Christianity-Brochure-Rad-Zdero.

CHAPTER 7

1. David Kinnaman and Gabe Lyons, "Unchristian: Change the Perception," *Q: Ideas for the Common Good*, http://www.qideas.org/essays/unchristian-change-the-perception.aspx.

2. George Barna, Perspectives letter "New Direction," April 2005 .

3. Rainie, Susannah Fox and Janna Anderson, "The Future of the Internet I," *PewResearch Internet Project*, January 9, 2005, http://www.pewinternet.org/2005/01/09/the-future-of-the-internet-i/.

4. David Eikenberry in Clayton Hardiman, "Final Answer: Survey says Bible Literacy Slipping," *Religion News Service*, April 12, 2001, http://amarillo.com/stories/2001/04/12/bel_slipping.shtml.

5. Gordon Marcy, "Has Internet Evangelism Reached the Tipping Point?" *Church Central*, April 23, 2012, http://www.churchcentral.com/blog/7819/Has-Internet-Evangelism-Reached-the-Tipping-Point.

Plan a Digital Outreach Focus Spot for Your Church or Group,"

Internet Evangelism Day, http://www.internetevangelismday.
com/planning.php.

CHAPTER 8

1. "Purpose Driven Life: Can Rick Warren Change the World?"
   Fox News, August 21, 2006, http://www.foxnews.com/
   story/2006/08/21/purpose-driven-life-can-rick-warren-change-
   world/.

2. Gary Kreps in Rainie and Anderson, "The Future of the Internet
   III," *PewResearch Internet Project*, December 14, 2008, http://
   www.pewinternet.org/2008/12/14/the-future-of-the-internet-
   iii/.

3. Paul D. Watson, "Losing the Online Generation," *Reaching
   the Online Generation*, September 1, 2010, http://www.
   reachingtheonlinegeneration.com/2010/09/01/losing-the-
   online-generation/.

4. David Kueker, "Four Systemic Problems in Disciple Making,"
   http://www.disciplewalk.com/files/Lecture_Unit_1_Kueker_
   Four_Systemic_Problems.pdf.

5. Beth HaDerech, "Become Like Our Rabbi Yeshua," March 29,
   2012.

6. Kevin Webb, "72 Percent of African-American Children Are
   Raised in Single Parent Homes," Atlanta Blackstar, December
   23, 2012, http://atlantablackstar.com/2012/12/23/72-percent-
   of-african-american-children-are-raised-in-single-parent-
   homes/.

7. Paul Taylor and Scott Keeter, eds., "Millennials, A Portrait of
   Generation Next," Pew Research Center, February 2010,
   http://www.pewsocialtrends.org/files/2010/10/millennials-
   confident-connected-open-to-change.pdf.

8. Ibid.

9. Ed Lyell in Anderson and Rainie, "The Future of Higher Education," *PewResearch Internet Project*, July 27, 2012, http://www.pewinternet.org/2012/07/27/the-future-of-higher-education/.

10. Cyndy Woods-Wilson in Anderson and Rainie, "The Future of Higher Education."

CHAPTER 9

1. President Harry S. Truman, letter to his wife, Bess, Sunday, May 7, 1933, http://www.trumanlibrary.org/whistlestop/study_collections/personal/large/folder2/trans050733.htm.

2. "Tracking Online Life: How Women Use the Internet to Cultivate Relationships with Family and Friends," *PewResearch Internet Project*, May 10, 2000, http://www.pewinternet.org/2000/05/10/tracking-online-life-how-women-use-the-internet-to-cultivate-relationships-with-family-and-friends/.

3. Jeffrey Boase, John B. Horrigan, Barry Wellman and Lee Rainie, "The Strength of Internet Ties: The Internet and Email Aid Users in Maintaining Their Social Networks and Provide Pathways to Help When People Face Big Decisions," Pew Internet and American Life Project, January 25, 2006, http://www.pewinternet.org/files/old-media/Files/Reports/2006/PIP_Internet_ties.pdf.pdf.

4. Personal interview with Laura Bradford, 2006.

5. "Most Churches Did Not Answer the Phone," Barna Group, January 26, 2004, https://www.barna.org/barna-update/article/5-barna-update/134-most-churches-did-not-answer-the-phone#.Uw6ZkIWLVsU.

CHAPTER 11

1. Pope Francis, *Evangelii Guadium 87* (Washington DC: USCCB, 2013).